MW01620874

ANDREW MARTIN

Int Des Rev Vol 12

Martin Waller
Daisy Bridgewater

Physiognomy is the science of reading people's personalities from their faces. It sounds superficial and simplistic. How can the essence of character and a lifetime of experience be so easily understood from a template that is fundamentally the product of inheritance?

Nevertheless we rely on this technique all the time. We do it in the most banal situations like choosing the person to sit next to on the bus. Then we use it in the most life changing ways such as choosing a partner for the next 50 years. There is some quirk in a face that is immediately appealing or decidedly unattractive.

In just the same way homes are a window on the personality of the owner. Their preferences and prejudices are betrayed in a myriad of different ways. Notice how books or shoes are stored and it reveals which has the higher priority. The austerity of minimalism and the clutter of collections describe their owners as surely as their faces.

It is the task of the designer to capture the essence of their client's personality and translate it into the interior. Of course the designer's style will also be apparent. But it should be equivalent to a biographer's technique. However admirable and elegant the writing, the biographical subject is what the book is about. This is why the most important quality in a designer is empathy. Listening and understanding are critical skills.

I am often asked how to choose an interior designer. My answer is always: pick someone you like and who likes you. On the other hand it's instructive to remember that the Aristotelian treatise Physiognomonica maintained that people with facial characteristics resembling certain animals have the temperaments ascribed to those animals. So designers shouldn't forget to check out the kennel.

Martin Waller

Kit Kemp

Designer: Kit Kemp.
Company: Firmdale Hotels, London.
Profile: Kit Kemp is the owner (along with husband Tim) and design director of Firmdale Hotels which comprises of 7 boutique hotels in London. Their most recent, Haymarket Hotel, opened in May 2007.

Kit is a high cheek boned awa
sense of colour and an apprec
She works from a 19th centur
swimming pool in the garden
office and finds that her staff
is holding a packet of biscuits

d-winner with an uninhibited
ation of cluttered minimalism.
London townhouse with a
vhich she refuses to call an
esponds best to her when she

Choosing carpets is perhaps her
in pink furry boots, she longs to
hair down to her waist, and som

life's biggest burden. At her best
ook like Doris Lessing with grey
times cries in the shower.

Jan des Bouvrie

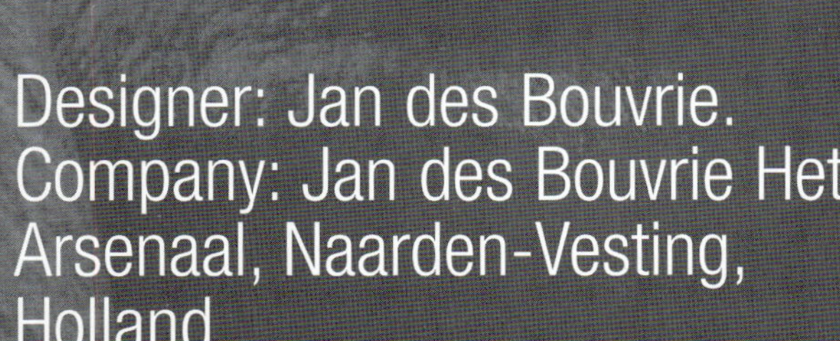

Designer: Jan des Bouvrie.
Company: Jan des Bouvrie Het Arsenaal, Naarden-Vesting, Holland.
Profile: Private residential projects and product design for big international brands. Current projects include the interior of a yacht, and the architecture and interior design of an apartment in Rotterdam.

A workaholic father of four who has just bo
reckons that the most important thing in lif
he struggles with English but has an impre
design. Delighted that his youngest daught
as he did, he sees creativity in all of his br

ght himself an Alfa Romeo C8, Jan
is to be happy on the inside. A jazz lover,
ive command of product and furniture
is now studying at the Rietveld Academy,
d and perfection in nobody.

Erin Martin

Designer: Erin Martin.
Company: Martin Design, St Helena, California.
Profile: A small company which often behaves like a large group, whose clients often appear in commercials. Current projects include a celebrity hideaway in the Napa Valley and a ski lodge near Beaver Creek, Colorado.

For Erin, decorating is not brain surgery, though it can sometimes feel like it. At the rate she is going, ten years from now she expects to find herself in a well-designed padded cell. Particularly partial to a client who pays, she sees herself as part nanny, part cottage industry, and likes people to high five when she walks into a room. Perfection is an in-house shrink, hot tamales and champagne. She thinks that the word 'budget' should be removed from the design world and that the caverns of her mind are the most beautiful place she has ever visited. Still recovering from being forced to play the cow bells in a rock 'n' roll band, she has no intention of living beyond 50.

Zaha Hadid

Designer: Zaha Hadid.
Company: Zaha Hadid Architects, London.
Profile: A company comprising of 200 architects and 30 support staff with site offices in Rome, Zaragoza and Guangzhou which is currently working on around 50 projects globally. These include the Aquatic Centre for the London 2012 Olympic Games, Opera Houses in Dubai and China, private houses in Moscow and the USA and major planning projects in Bilbao, Istanbul and the Middle East.

With a belief that all buildings deserve to be interesting, Zaha Hadid is committed to constructions which evoke experiences akin to the strangeness and newness of visiting a country for the first time. Unafraid of dedicating vast amounts of time and energy to achieving the desired effect, she reckons that in 10 years time she will be designing an entire district of a city. Deeply inspired by the landscape of Southern Iraq, her architecture is still trying to capture that seamless flow between the sand, the water and the wildlife, but in an urban context for a city and its users. Experimental, dedicated, occasionally crazy, she sees the enlightened open-mindedness of her parents as the key to her success.

Douglas Mackie

Designer: Douglas Mackie.
Company: D Mackie Design Ltd, London.
Profile: A small company dealing in private residential projects internationally. Recent work includes apartments in central London and a Grade I listed house in Norfolk; current projects include a house in Notting Hill and an apartment in New York.

Felix Nussbaum

An aesthetic editor with a taste for expensive toast, Douglas is getting wiser every day. Insisting on scrupulous manners and writerly emails, it is only in his dreams that he allows himself to be bad. A Francophile at ease with his own perfection, he cites modesty as his best feature and would not consider tampering with what Nature has given him. Usually to be found in a hand-made Neapolitan jacket paired with worn out jeans, he plays the violin like an angel and dreams of eating raw sea urchins with his wife in the South of France.

Aleksandra Laska

Designer: Aleksandra Laska.
Company: Ola Laska, Warsaw, Poland.
Profile: A freelance designer working mainly in Poland for private clients, and on show apartments for large development firms. Recent work includes the dressing rooms and part of the foyer of the Opera House in Warsaw, while current work includes an apartment in London's Chelsea Harbour, and the reconstruction and redecoration of an apartment in Warsaw.

An intuitive ocean lover who likes to take her compliments from the stars, Aleksandra would rather not rush things. A night owl who is ageing rather well, she puts her good posture down to a talent for dancing, and wishes that everybody with whom she works would wear see-through clothes. Happiest on the dance floor, and frequently to be found crying with laughter, she maintains a childish curiosity for the world and considers messiness a delight to the imagination.

ARTE OGGI
ARTE OGGI

Fiona Barratt

Designer: Fiona Barratt.
Company: Fiona Barratt Interiors, London.
Profile: A mixture of commercial and domestic projects all over the world. New projects include houses in Santa Monica and Quinta do Lago, Portugal. Completed projects include The Lodge, in Verbier Switzerland, one of Richard Branson's Limited Edition Virgin Hotels.

Blue-eyed offspring of the Barratt Homes dynasty, Fiona is well schooled in how to build a successful business. Toying with the idea of a taupe tracksuit for site installations, she sees nothing but expansion in the future, particularly with Richard Branson as her first (highly satisfied) client. Waking to a mental list of everything that she has to achieve that day, she does not do clutter and likes appliances that do what they say on the box.

For Fiona, paradise is a tossup betwe
horse ride through the dewy Northum
either, so long as she can eat brown

n a tall and toned boyfriend, and a
erland countryside. She will settle for
ead and salted butter afterwards.

Brian Glückstein

Designer: Brian Gluckstein.
Company: Gluckstein Design Planning Inc, Toronto.
Profile: High end interior design, planning and project management for residential and corporate clients.

Firm but flexible, Brian insists that he is just doing what he loves most. Happiest head to toe in oatmeal cashmere, he knows that he should take more exercise but claims his lack of interest in the gym is beyond his control. Gripped by a serious book habit that took hold when he read Charlie and the Chocolate Factory as a boy. Governed by friendship, and aggravated by clutter, he loves nothing better than his ability to be life-changing.

Angelos Angelopoulos

Designer: Angelos Angelopoulos.
Company: Angelos Angelopoulos, Athens, Greece.
Profile: A wide range of projects from private houses and apartment blocks to boutique hotels. Recent work includes private residences in Greece and Cyprus.

Angelos is a Kimono wearer w
who has already submitted hin
With a desire to improve his in
remembered as a conscious m
unspeakable things he did in h

an environmental conscience
elf to the surgeon's knife.

er-self, he would like to be
n, and to forget all of the
youth.

Believing in democracy in the office, he has a 2 hour rule for meetings and a deep respect for deadlines. Travelling almost without respite, he dreams of flying and of being covered in talcum powder, in no particular order.

Amanda Kaye and Lisa McCartney

Designers: Amanda Kaye and Lisa McCartney.
Company: LK Interiors, Hertfordshire, UK.
Profile: International company specialising in domestic projects. Recent work includes an 8 bedroom villa in Umbria, Italy and a Grade II listed 12 bedroom house in Hertfordshire. Current work includes an apartment in London's Canary Wharf and a restaurant and private dining room in Hertfordshire.

Female intuition, personal connection, and a ni
success. Collectively neither thin nor tall enoug
are most comfortable in their pyjamas and mat

cup of tea are the key to Amanda and Lisa's
hey dream of plane crashes and tooth loss and
ng company slippers eating macaroni cheese.

Taught by their grandparents that cigarettes and alcohol will not necessarily kill them, they would like to shut their eyes and transport themselves to Disney World, though they claim to be maturing with age. Self-professed clean queens, they worship at the altar of the vacuum cleaner and wish everyone would stop using the word 'eclectic'. If ever they win the Lottery they will hold a tarts and vicars party at the Pantheon.

Philip Tang & Brian Ip

Designers: Philip Tang & Brian Ip.
Company: P.Tang Studio Ltd, Hong Kong.
Profile: Design studio of ten dealing in high end residential and commercial projects, located mainly in Hong Kong and mainland China. Recent work includes a 3-storey house in Fei Ngo Shan in Hong Kong and an executive office in Shanghai, China.

A couple of nice guys who like their job, Philip and Brian prefer the type of client who settles their bill promptly. Philip cut his design teeth on a public lavatory in Hong Kong, and plans to build a similar creation underneath the Great Wall of China. Happiest in his own company, Brian is dreaming up plans for a pet hotel in Hong Kong, and reckons that life is sweeter in Manhattan. Surgically attached to his Tag Heuer watch, he fantasises about Tyra Bank's bedroom. Philip could do with growing a few inches, though his obsession with computer games might stunt him further.

Sandra Nunnerley

Designer: Sandra Nunnerley.
Company: Sandra Nunnerley, New York.
Profile: High end residential interior design firm which also takes on select commercial projects like boutique hotels and private clubs. Previous work includes the interior of a private plane, and the interior of a house in Lyford Cay in the Bahamas. Current work includes a ski chalet in Aspen, Colorado and an apartment in the new Robert Stern building in Manhattan.

Sandra is mistress of a good taste empire over which she rules with a silken whip. For her, jeans are not always appropriate, and hat wearing impossible. Best in the mornings after she has had a chance to sleep on things, she longs to be a Bond Girl with long, golden, flowing hair and dreads walking into a room with no coffee. At her best barefoot in a fountain, at her worst perusing paperback fiction, she has still not got over being forbidden from playing the electric guitar as a child, and still harbours a desire to be Marianne Faithful. Fascinated by other people's habits, she longs to get inside Donald Trump's living room and give him a lesson in refinement.

Sue Rohrer

Designer: Sue Rohrer.
Company: Sue Rohrer SA, Zurich, Switzerland.
Profile: Mostly residential work in Europe, the USA and Dubai; currently working on a villa in Zurich and estates in Ibiza and the South of France.

Champagne loving, Prada wearing former shop owner who believes that in design, less is more, and that a designer should leave space for a client's personal belongings. When it comes to her domestic life she cannot wait to get her hands on her husband's attic where he hoards his clutter. She has a garden which is magical at night, a profound love of India, and an affinity with horses. Busiest in the hours before midnight.

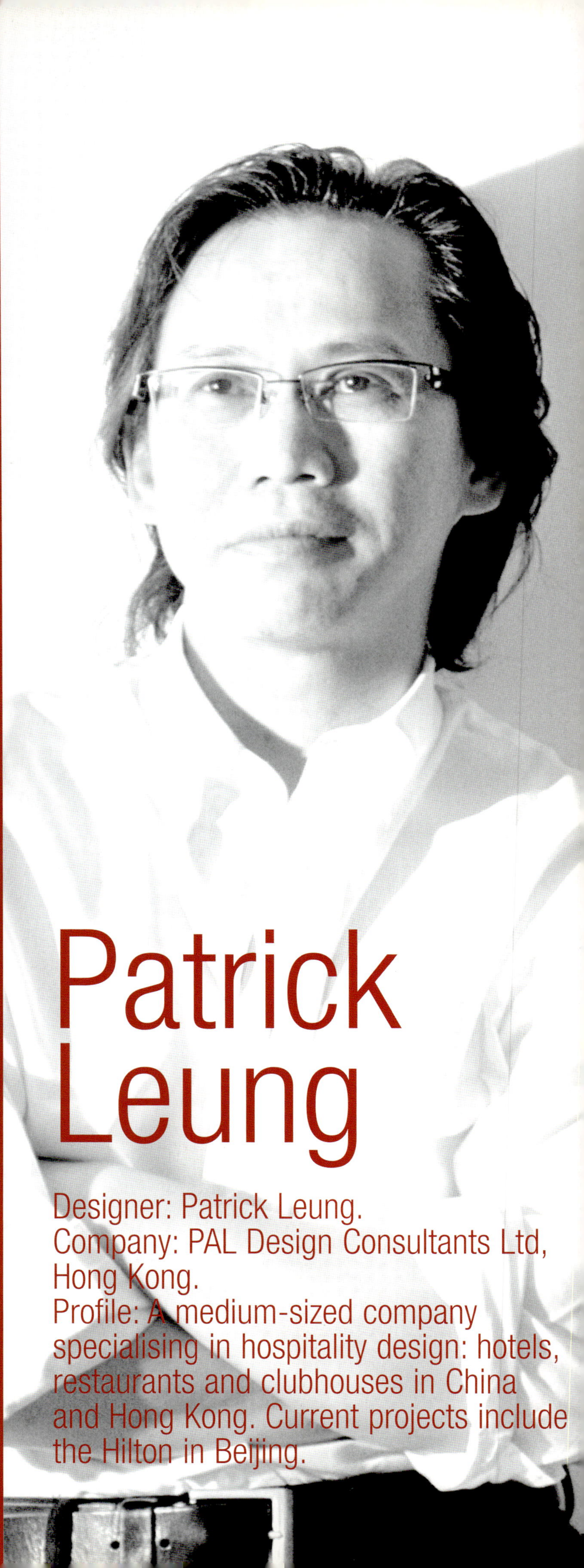

Patrick Leung

Designer: Patrick Leung.
Company: PAL Design Consultants Ltd, Hong Kong.
Profile: A medium-sized company specialising in hospitality design: hotels, restaurants and clubhouses in China and Hong Kong. Current projects include the Hilton in Beijing.

A stranger to the computer, Patrick prefers to do things longhand, preferably in scratchy red biro. As a stickler for time keeping, he would love to put office late-comers into detention, as a professional he dreads too many requests for work. Freely admitting to having designed the biggest golf club in the world, he equates happiness with a hole in one and has not cried for 15 years. Unclear as to whether his schoolboy nickname, Fatboy, has stuck, he dreams of a little more height and has forgotten the name of his favourite teacher.

Natallia Fiadchuk

Designer: Natallia Fiadchuk.
Company: Geometry, Moscow, Russia.
Profile: Both private and public projects, including cafes, restaurants and offices, and which also produces a range of furniture and lamps. Recent projects include the award-winning GQ Bar in Moscow and various private houses and apartments.

Modest, thoughtful, caring: Natallia thinks that the psychological well-being of her staff will translate itself into the harmony of a project. She believes in virgin colours, good interpretation, and in design being meaningful as a whole. As a child she would search through shredded fabrics to make clothes for her dolls.

Saving her tears for her dreams, she says that her heightened sensibility is genetic and that her three children are as independent and sensitive as she is. For Natallia, inspiration came during rhythmic gymnastics when every prop and costume was made by hand. Bewitched by absolute beauty, she has been known to find it at the bottom of her garden.

Nick and Christian Candy

Designers: Nick and Christian Candy.
Company: Candy & Candy, Knightsbridge, London.
Profile: Interior designers and property developers with headquarters in Knightsbridge and a second office on Rodeo Drive, Beverly Hills. The company offers a complete, bespoke lifestyle experience, be it the design of a luxury apartment or the interior of a super-yacht.

As trail blazing brothers who strive perpetually to improve, Nick and Christian credit themselves with changing London's skyline for the better. Working from desks which face each other to cut out the emails and telephone calls, both like to tackle problems head on and blame their obsessive attention to detail on their father. Nick came to design via accountancy and has the ability to sleep well anywhere. Admitting to increasing everyone's workload the moment he walks into the office, he likes nothing less than a cluttered desk, believing it makes it impossible to work effectively. Whilst uniforms are discouraged in the office, they are working on a little something for the crew members of their yacht, Candyscape II.

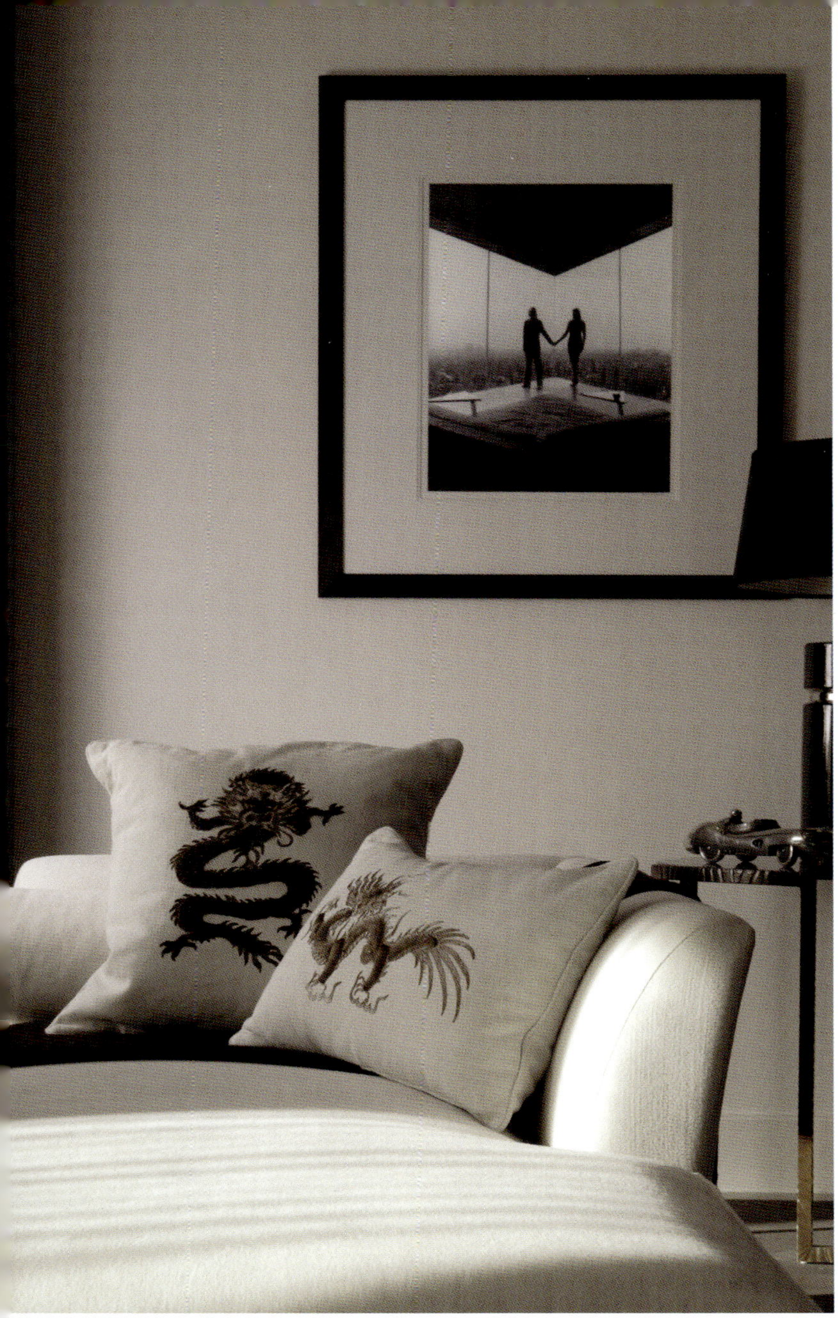

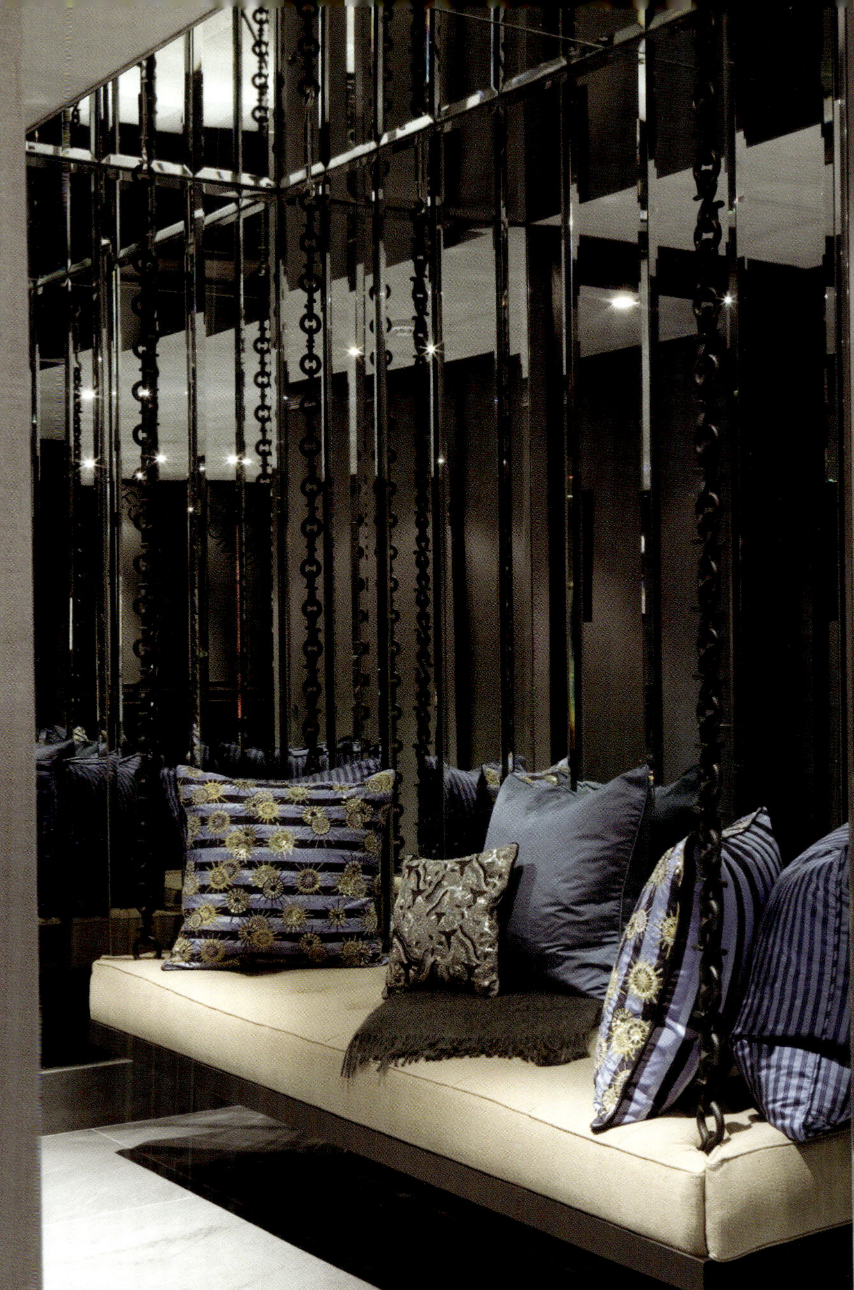

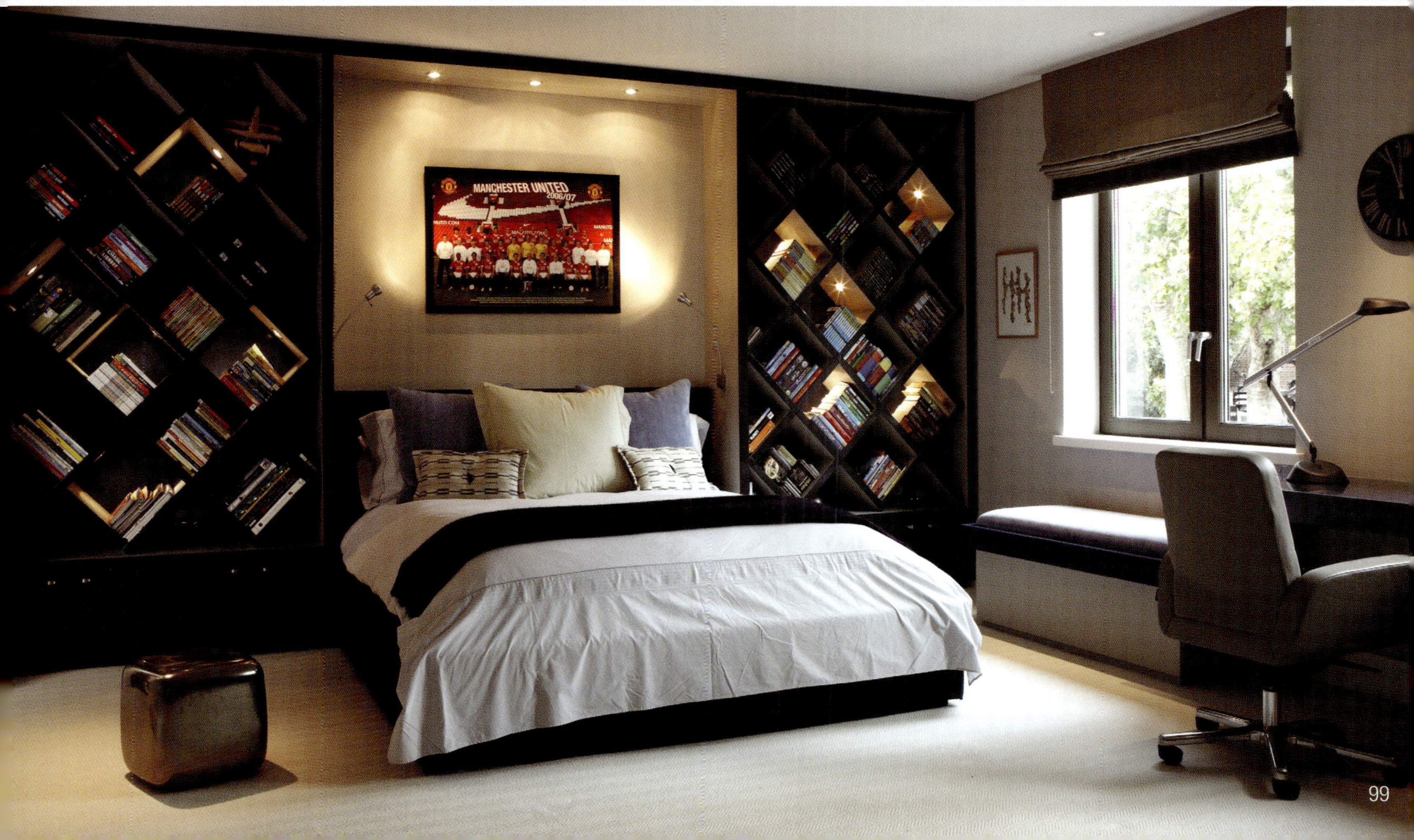
MANCHESTER UNITED
2006/07

Giano Gonçalves

Designer: Giano Gonçalves.
Company: Ana D'Arfet, Funchal, Madeira.
Profile: Most projects are in Madeira or on mainland Portugal, and comprise hotels, restaurants and private houses. Recent work includes golf club houses on Porto Santo Island and Madeira.

A volatile designer with a penchant for leather aprons and a love of abundance, Giano believes that a tan is the answer to most of his body anxieties. With his sea blue eyes and tuxedo shirt, he is happiest contemplating the ocean or flying in his dreams. Demanding uncompromising loyalty from his staff, he finds himself losing his temper in the office one minute, and telling everybody he loves them the next. As a child he asked his grandmother to marry him and learnt to play Beethoven on the piano over the telephone. Just thinking of his babies makes him weep.

CENTURY
MILLERS
TOMAS TAVEIRA
CUBA
NACIONAL
Rothmans
Colecção Berardo
ROSA CARVALHO
Marlboro

madeira
GOLFE

Worth Interiors

Designers: Eddy Doumas, Dana Hugo and Lisa Kanning.
Company: Worth Interiors, Avon, Colorado, USA.
Profile: Mainly residential projects, with the occasional design-driven commercial project. Current projects include a large ranch home in Montana, a home in the hills outside San Francisco, and an apartment in Manhattan.

Eddy is a creative powerhouse with a cool head for business who is harbouring the desire to create a commune of good taste. Most productive in the shower, or with a cocktail in his hand, he believes that good design requires a certain passion, and that budgets are almost always unrealistic. Dreading anyone else telling him they are pregnant, he has banned raspberry tea and eggs from the office, and is still haunted by his old boss after 14 years. Dana can already picture herself travelling by private jet, but for now she is still tortured by spam emails and filing. She blames her mother for her bad hair and nails, but still fantasises about sharing an office with George Clooney. Pity anyone who stands in the way of broad-shouldered Lisa; she has forbidden anyone in the office from arguing with her and her last assistant only lasted 2 days. Saddened by the death of her 20 year old cat, cheered by the thought of plastic surgery, and committed to at least another ten years of hard grafting, she likes nothing better than a client who is ready to learn.

EARTH
ANIMAL
OCEAN
rainforest
SPACE
HUMAN
PLANT

Flora Lau

Designer: Flora Lau.
Company: Flora Lau Designers Company, Hong Kong.
Profile: Small interior design consultancy working in China on mainly commercial projects, including clubhouses, hotels and show homes.

Highly principled, happiest at church, and with designs on heaven, Flora would like to be remembered as a good Christian. Keen on cats, she would love to build an animal rescue centre in China, and a concrete church for celebrities to visit. She finds clutter safe and peaceful, uses her window box for storage, and considers her tender heart her only vice.

ABCDEFGHIJKLMNOPQRSTUVWXYZ

Jan Showers

Designer: Jan Showers.
Company: Jan Showers & Associates, Dallas, Texas.
Profile: High end residential design predominantly in the USA. Current work includes a penthouse at the Ritz Carlton in Dallas and an estate in Austin, Texas.

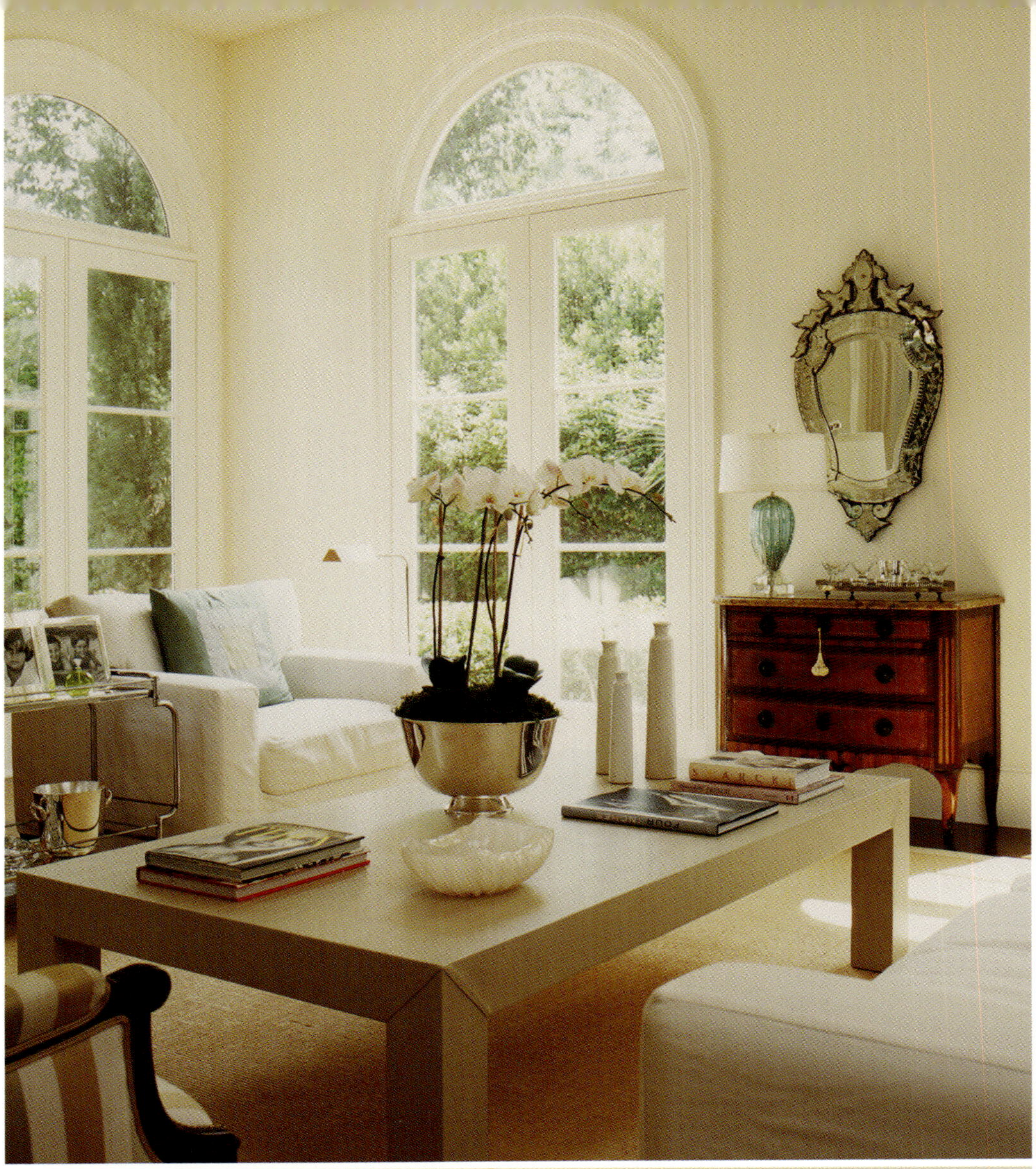

THE ORCHID

audrey hepburn
ART GLASS FROM MURANO

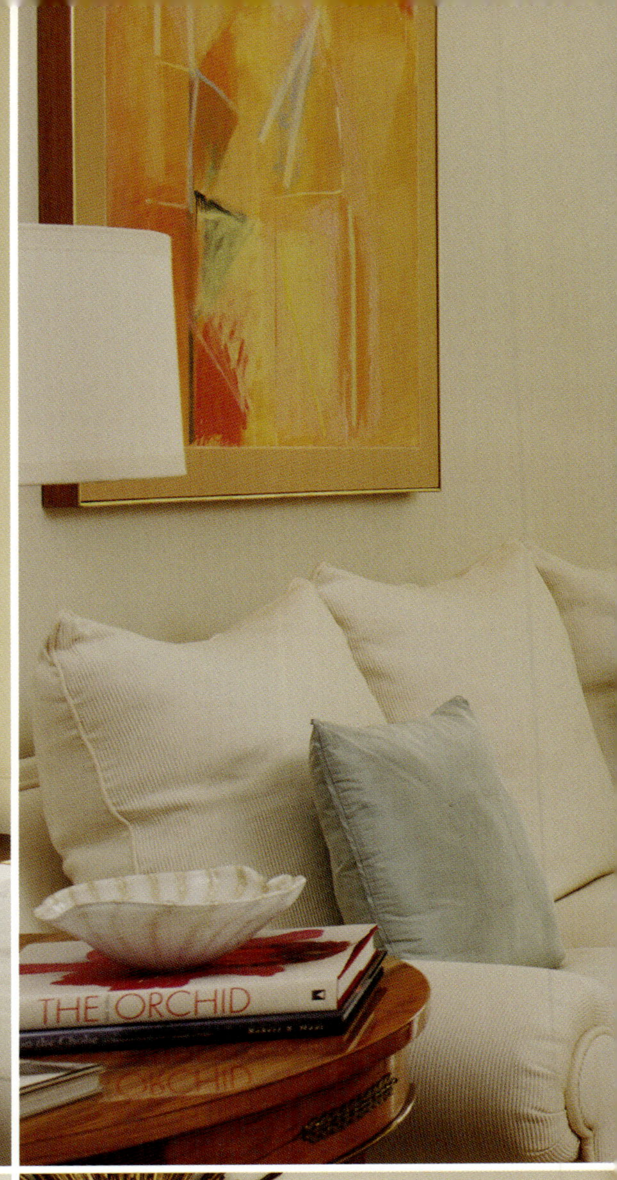

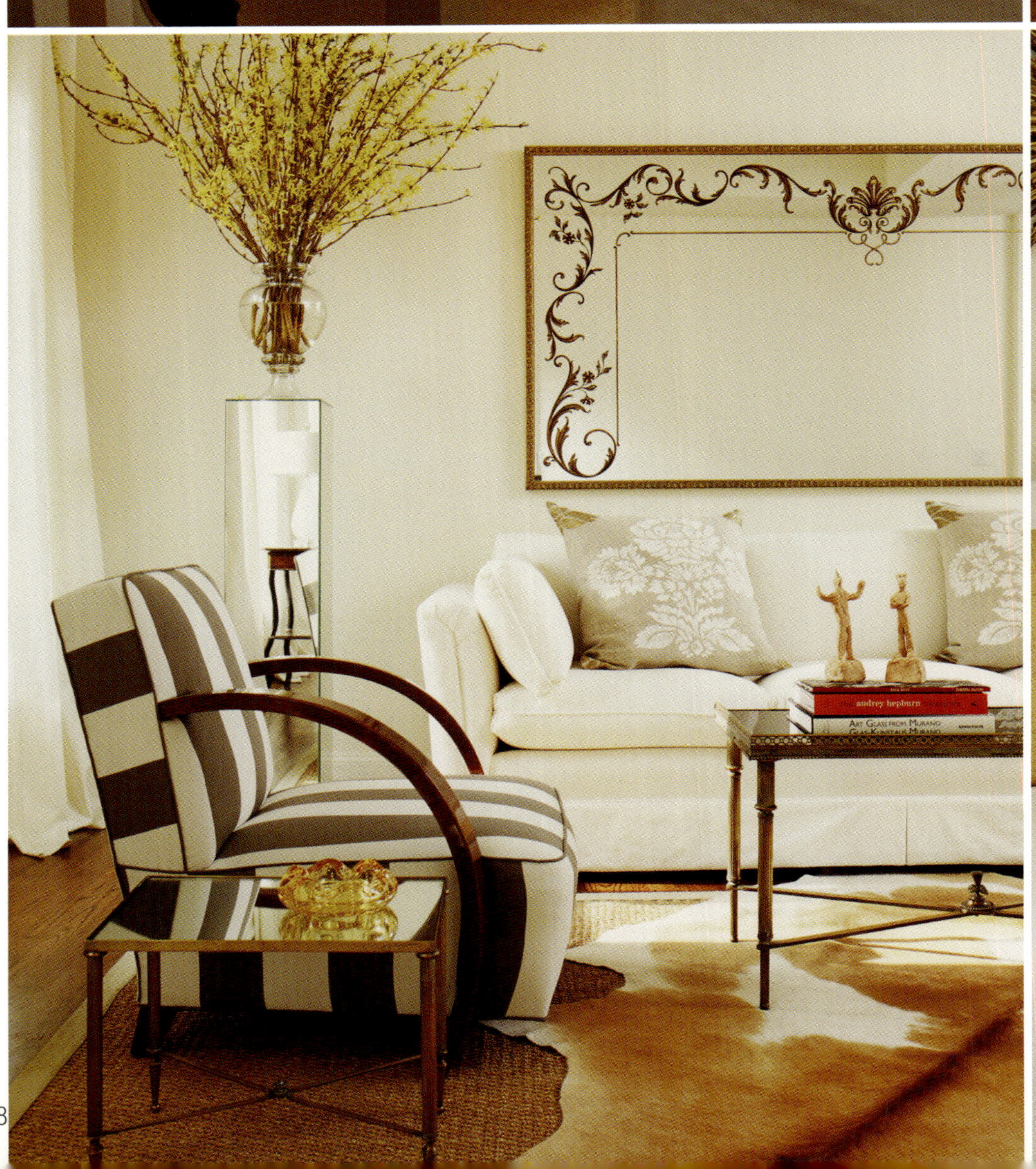

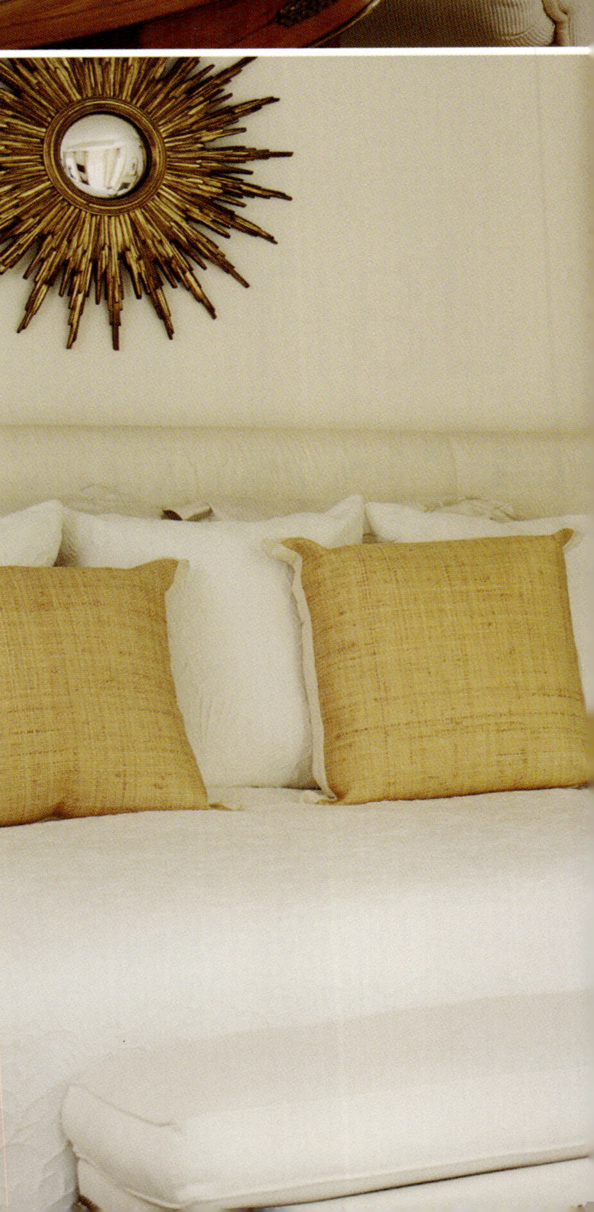

MARK ROTHKO
110
BERT STERN ADVENTURES
MAASAI

An unintentional empire builder, after 25 years on the job Jan now has an interior design business, a large antiques showroom and a furniture making business, not to mention a book in the offing. With her radar in good working order she selects clients by instinct and likes to think that she is enriching their lives. Never short on compliments, she says she has a marvellous, motivated staff whose outfits she looks forward to admiring every day. With the intention of ageing gracefully, and with a keen desire for longer legs, she will always cry at the end of Dr Zhivago, and swears that one day she will do more charity work.

Stefano Dorata

Designer: Stefano Dorata.
Company: Stefano Dorata Architetto, Rome, Italy.
Profile: Studio comprised of architects and designers, working chiefly on private houses and hotels. Recent work includes a mountain hut in Cortina d'Ampezzo, a loft in Marsiglia and an apartment in Milan.

An early rising man of simple pleasures, Stefano has a calm, uncomplicated belief in beautiful houses, and an uncompromising disdain for bureaucracy. No wiser now than he was at five, he will still be wedded to his pencil in 10 years time, at which point he will still be choosing which of this world's many monstrosities he would like to demolish first. Having run with the bulls in Pamplona, he now has his sights set on redecorating George Michael's house and on transforming the Kremlin into an upmarket hotel.

live woman
than a
Leopard

LUXU

Kunihide Oshinomi

Designer: Kunihide Oshinomi.
Company: K/O Design Studio, Tokyo, Japan.
Profile: Private studio working predominantly in Japan on an extremely wide range of projects, from the design of a small chair to a skyscraper. Current work includes a condominium design project in a seaside town in Japan, and the design of a showroom for a kitchen company in Tokyo.

A self-confessed design ac
for the perfect state of bei
Most productive in the ear
about working from a trave
be found wearing Dior Hor

ct on a permanent quest
J.

evening, he fantasises
ng studio and is mostly to
ne.

A subscriber to the National Geographic, he dreams of escaping to Africa and dreads his assistants not showing up for work.

With a healthy dislike of restrictions and rules he has decided to postpone building his empire.

For the time being, anyway.

Dina El Khachab and Hedayat Islam

Designers: Dina El Khachab and Hedayat Islam.
Company: Eklego Design Ltd, Cairo.
Profile: Architectural interior and furniture design firm with over 80 projects all over Egypt which range from private residences to retail spaces, restaurants and commercial offices. Recent projects include extensive work in the Red Sea resorts of Sharm El Sheikh and El Gouna, and the design of the first outlet of a chain of gourmet food stores in Egypt.

Hedayat is an interior designer who likes to keep things simple and functional; Dina is an architect who cannot tolerate unnecessary questions. Between them they admit to too many office rules and a wish to build an empire. Sometimes greeted with panic-stricken faces when she walks into the office, Hedayat shudders at the thought of unmet deadlines and dreams of switching jobs with a pastry chef. Dina heeds her grandmother's advice that if you lose something, it is a waste of time looking for it as it will appear on its own. Hedayat has a love of excess, burgers and Quaker oats; Dina has a serious sugar habit and admits her social life could do with some input. Both would like to throw a party at the train station in Cairo.

A young, ambitious mother of four with big ideas about lifestyle, Maria likes a client who is willing to give up control. Happiest with a glass of Diet Coke in her hand listening to the slow chug of boats in her summer home, she dreams of publishing a book on everything from laying a table to throwing a party. Taught to shop, to dress up, and to love city life by her grandmother, she cannot tolerate the term 'East meets West'.

Maria Hovtun

Designer: Maria E. N. Hovtun.
Company: Maria Interior Design, Oslo, Norway.
Profile: An individual working in partnership with other architects, designing luxury homes for private clients predominantly in Norway. Recent projects include a mountain lodge in Norefjell and a summer house in Oslofjord. She is currently working on the rebuild and redecoration of her own home.

Tall, smiley, a tendency to cry, she has learnt to tolerate her children's clutter and would like to wake up every morning to a slice of bread and butter with home-made jam.

Associates III

Designer: Kari Foster.
Company: Associates III Interior Design, Denver, USA.
Profile: A group of 15 female designers working on residential, hospitality and resort projects predominantly around Colorado and the Rocky Mountains region, with a strong focus on environmental sensitivity. Recent work includes a mountain resort and several eco-friendly luxury mountain homes.

As Principal Designer, cowboyboot wearing Kari Foster is a green-minded visionary who has written a hefty tome and has a fear of being buried alive by emails. Senior Designer Maggie Tandysh gets her kicks from creating life and Earth enhancing homes and from working amongst similarly dynamic women. Project Designer Rachael Morton used to be a professional salsa dancer. It was her grandparents who taught her how to hold a pencil. Nathalie Lynch, also a project designer, is happiest in the springtime and has already planted a vegetable patch in her mind.

Kris Lin

Designer: Kris Lin.
Company: KLID, Shanghai.
Profile: Predominantly commercial design in China, including show flats, offices and clubs.

A fearless, free-styling former hip-hop dancer, today Kris is most comfortable in a suit and wishes that he didn't have to travel so much. With fantasies of playing professional baseball, and plans to eat his last supper at McDonald's, he would like to throw a party in the Forbidden City and then relocate to Switzerland.

КРАСОТА
В ИЗГНАНИИ

Nadia & Georgy Ananiev

Designers: Nadia & Georgy Ananiev.
Company: ABL Architecture & Design Bureau, Moscow.
Profile: Predominantly the design of private apartments in Russia, with the occasional commercial project.

Brought up on illustrated Russian fairy tales, these former artists have their eye on a future empire, and would like to think that they are both rather mesmerizing. In their dreams they would design a museum of snow in a country where it never freezes. Old age will mean eating grilled fish with their future grandchildren at a riverside dacha. Georgy likes nothing more than the smell of the thawed ground in the springtime; Nadia likes to be woken by the cat's meow and the sound of the shower. Standing in the sea of dandelions that is their garden, neither can decide if they want to be sultans or singers.

Kathleen Hay

Designer: Kathleen Hay.
Company: Kathleen Hay Designs, Nantucket, USA.
Profile: A self-consciously small company specialising in high end residential projects with an emphasis on new construction. Recent work includes a summer estate on the island of Nantucket, a pied a terre in Palm Beach and a luxury duplex in New York City.

A spunky caffeine addict with a morbid fear of doctors, Kathleen spends her days avoiding clutter like the plague. For her the office is refuge, punctuality crucial and paperwork purgatory. Slightly shorter than her ideal, she is at ease in a dress with a good pair of boots, and happiest in possession of a Kir Royale (preferably in Paris). Emerging from a youth too crazy to revisit she has resolved to do more exercise and design a country house in Ireland. The Best of Van Morrison gets her out of bed; the smell of chalk takes her back to her school days when she was old before her time.

Joseph Sy

Designer: Joseph Sy.
Company: Joseph Sy & Associates, Hong Kong.
Profile: Residential and commercial projects in Hong Kong, China and the Philippines.

Joseph is a wavy-haired fishing enthusiast who is ageing artistically. Haunted by dreams of being weighed down by his own legs, he was nicknamed Flying Pen at school and accused of being absent-minded.

Arriving unnoticed every day in an office where common sense is the only rule, he feels that recognition is his biggest professional success.

Daun Curry & Nicole Fuller

Designers: Daun Curry and Nicole Fuller.
Company: Vessper Wilde, New York.
Profile: Boutique firm offering high end residential and commercial design services. Recent work includes a penthouse triplex, a triangular loft and a modern townhouse, all in New York City.

Nicole is a twilight thinker who finds it hard to sit up straight. Happiest when a client says 'yes' to everything, she would like to dress her staff in karate suits and share a desk with Michael Caine in a paper-free office. Daun dreams of flying like a bird and wakes up to the sound of her Blackberry. Devoid of any mentionable vices, she cannot tolerate the word 'juxtaposition' and will never forget Mrs Dean, her English teacher.

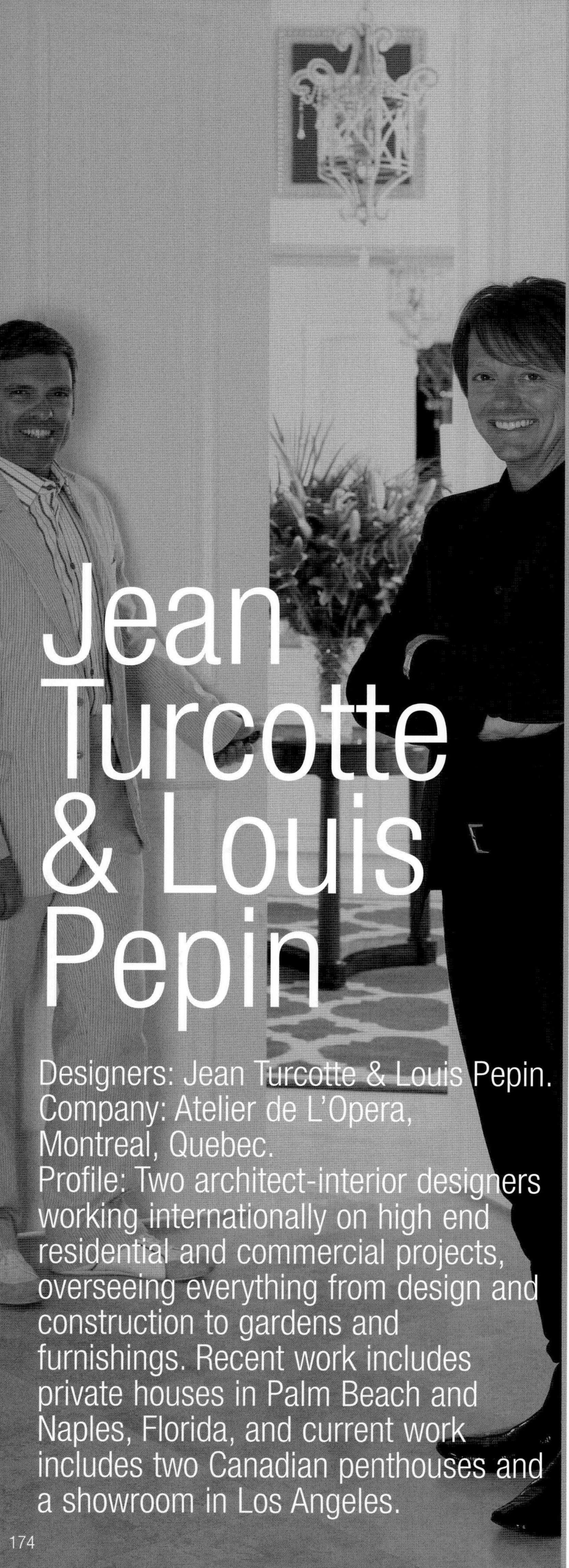

Jean Turcotte & Louis Pepin

Designers: Jean Turcotte & Louis Pepin.
Company: Atelier de L'Opera, Montreal, Quebec.
Profile: Two architect-interior designers working internationally on high end residential and commercial projects, overseeing everything from design and construction to gardens and furnishings. Recent work includes private houses in Palm Beach and Naples, Florida, and current work includes two Canadian penthouses and a showroom in Los Angeles.

Dressed in black, this elegant pair of wide-angled thinkers would like to go down in history for their passion for simplicity. Lacking the energy to change anything about their appearances, they value personality over beauty and would happily breakfast on summer fruits for the rest of their lives.

Patricia Pedrazzi

Designer: Patricia Pedrazzi.
Company: Innolink-Ambient, Lugano, Switzerland.
Profile: Company of five working on large residential projects, private houses, offices and yachts all over Europe, and in St Moritz, London and Paris in particular. Current projects include villas in St Tropez and Sardinia.

Committed, reliable, and most productive at sunset, Patricia designs houses like handmade dresses and has architecture in her DNA. Living in harmony with her clutter, she has free-range pigs and hens in her garden and admits to being terribly messy. She once laced an overfriendly stranger's drink with laxatives on a long haul flight, and she dreams of holding a wild party on the roof of the Vendramin Palace in Venice. Hooked on hot chocolate and the smell of the Sardinian maquis, she would like to design a playroom in a children's hospital, and is never happier than with her daughter, Jade.

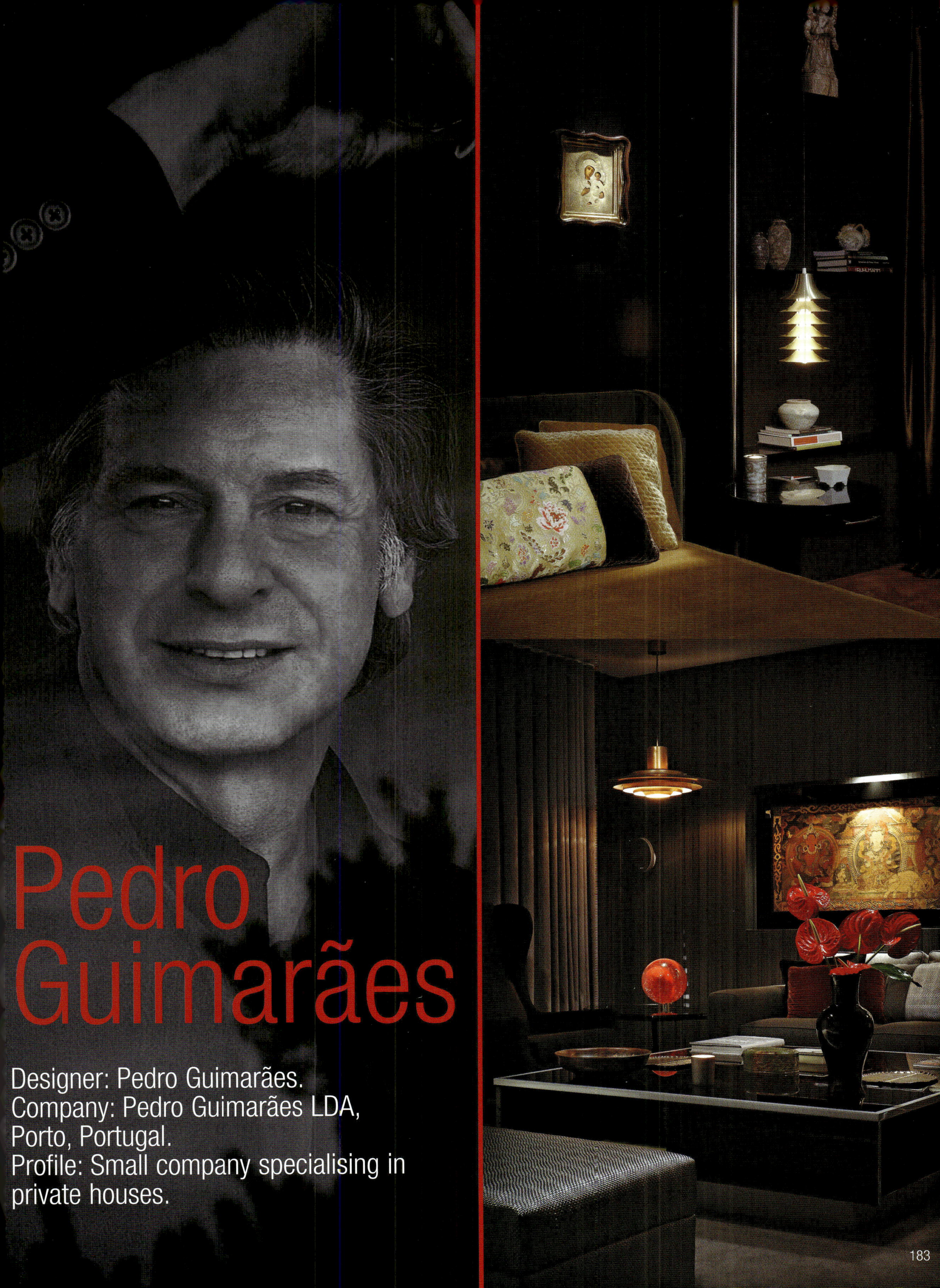

Pedro Guimarães

Designer: Pedro Guimarães.
Company: Pedro Guimarães LDA, Porto, Portugal.
Profile: Small company specialising in private houses.

This dignified don of deco 'design' is looking forwar passing on his business a Honoured by a retrospec

ting who loathes the word
to his retirement and to
d knowledge to his assistants.
e exhibition in Macau,

feted as one of Portugal's most influential interior decorators, he dreams about work and is at his most productive at night.

Colleagues call him 'Boss', he calls his maid a saint.

Ajax Law and Virginia Lung

Designers: Ajax Law and Virginia Lung.
Company: One Plus Partnership Ltd, Hong Kong.
Profile: Commercial design including club houses, cinemas and show apartments. Current projects include the Palace Cinema at the World Trade Centre in Beijing.

Ajax is conscientious, diligent and responsible; Virginia is passionate, sensitive and bold. Together they are a hive of activity in the early hours of the morning but worry constantly about their health. Happiest in bed, Ajax would like better skin and the chance to build something in the sky. Virginia would like to replace the Eiffel Tower and nominate herself for sainthood. Neither feels they have ever done anything crazy enough, though Ajax is planning a naked retirement party at the top of the Statue of Liberty.

Born to be a designer, Marta has been rearranging the furniture since she was a little girl, much to the distraction of her mother. Today she receives her best compliments from her own daughters and dreads nothing in life except unpaid invoices and the urge for another cigarette. Transported away by the smell of steel blades from antique silver knives, she wakes up to the sound of the sea and longs to teach the Brazilians a thing or two about decorating. In an ideal world she would give up smoking and have Harrison Ford as a client.

Marta Espregueira Mendes

Designer: Marta Espregueira Mendes.
Company: Marta's, Porto, Portugal.
Profile: Predominantly private projects internationally. Current projects include a private house in Oporto and a farm house at Viana do Castelo. Recent work includes offices for Volvo and Oporto Football Club.

Thomas Chan

Designer: Thomas Chan.
Company: Thomas Chan Designers Ltd, Hong Kong.
Profile: Two design offices, with a head office in Hong Kong and a branch office in China and a total staff of 60. Work is predominantly commercial and in China and Hong Kong. Current projects include a boutique hotel in Hainan, China, and the Cassina showroom in Hong Kong.

Thomas is a workaholic amate
awards in his cap and a long w
in jeans, proficient at spending
has never been happier in his

photographer with a string of
ing list of potential clients. Happiest
oney, and comfortably talented, he
than right now.

He would like to redesign the waiting room at his dentist to make his visits there more tolerable, and would happily breakfast on spicy Szechuan noodles and plum wine for the rest of his life.

As a child Luciana drew houses in the sand. At 15 she designed and built a beach house with her father. She has never looked back. Marked out as a future ballerina, she was sent to school in Ramsgate, Kent, but would never settle anywhere but Brazil. An amateur gardener and accomplished cook, she is reduced to tears by beauty and tales of misspent youth. Happy with her looks she would never consider plastic surgery, though she was once complimented on her work by one of Brazil's most eminent surgeons.

Luciana Teperman

Designer: Luciana Teperman.
Company: Luciana Teperman, Sao Paulo, Brazil.
Profile: Private residences around Brazil and internationally. Projects include various beach houses in Rio de Janeiro, two farm houses in the state of Sao Paulo and private apartments in Miami and New York.

VERANDA

Kiyofumi Yusa and Richard Lee

Designers: Kiyofumi Yusa and Richard Lee.
Company: R&K Partners Inc, Tokyo.
Profile: A company of nine carrying out a wide range of projects from large commercial to small residential work. Considered cinema, retail and restaurant experts in Japan, their work is in fact far more diverse; current projects include private houses, fitness clubs, offices and showrooms.

SCREEN 5.6.7.8

Richard likes to keep things rigorously simple and elegant. He does not have a need to get along with his clients; more a need for mutual respect. Most productive at midnight when the telephones stop ringing, he would like to build a monument to Einstein and relocate his office to the modern and minimal Arctic. By night he dreams of burning fire stations, by day he dresses in black and tries to cool his hot head with jazz and thoughts of Angelina Jolie in a halo. Kiyofumi is a chain smoking dreamer with a social conscience and an aversion to sashimi. He would like to work from a spaceship in a world where money has no value, replace the world's slums with parks, and remodel his entire body. Hot dogs with Clint Eastwood would be his dying wish.

Robert Walker

Designer: Robert Walker.
Company: Alexander James Interiors, Berkshire, UK.
Profile: High end residential projects. Recent work includes three show apartments in a converted Abbey and former boy's school in Berkshire, and the total refurbishment of a large country house in Surrey.

Despite the passion and precis
morning, as managing director
office ignoring him when he ar
as Captain Kirk might change
two sons he would like to nom
daughter is already an angel.

n Robert brings to work every
e longs to stop the rest of the
es. He imagines that dressing
ngs. As the proud father of
ate his wife for sainthood. His

With a deep appreciation of Le
to have Angelina Jolie at his b
forgotten the day that his fathe
designer, nor has that momen

Zeppelin, and a latent desire
k and call, he has never
won an Oscar as a production
inspiration ever left him.

Kinney Chan

Designer: Kinney Chan.
Company: Kinney Chan & Associates, Hong Kong.
Profile: International firm offering a broad spectrum of interior design projects from bar and restaurant design to private houses and show flats. Recent work includes the Tribeca club in Hong Kong and a show flat in Guangzhou.

Enter Kinney, a bearded wannabe
Armani and a desire to be as fam
inside. A little short-sighted, and
his work could be free of budgets
he was over-confident, although h
award by the Governor of Hong K
intends to be wiser at 100.

ck star with a taste for Giorgio
s outside Greater China as he is
rful of deadlines, he wishes that
s a child he was often told that
was once awarded a Boy Scout
g. His favourite food is toast. He

Jim Gauthier and Susan Stacy

Designers: Jim Gauthier and Susan Stacy.
Company: Gauthier Stacy Inc., Boston, USA.
Profile: Residential projects, plus the occasional resort and private club, throughout the USA. Recent work includes a penthouse on Fisher Island, a lakeside residence in Austin Texas, and the refurbishment of an antique commuter yacht.

A HISTORY OF ARCHITECTURE
WILLIAM WEGMAN PUPPIES
HISTORY OF ITALIAN RENAISSANCE ART
HOME BOOKS
EYE TO EYE LANTING

Jim is a serious listener with a chocolate Rolo habit who lets the voices in his head tell him if he is going to get on with a client. His colleagues may roll their eyes and giggle when he walks in, but Jim knows that he has a magician's touch and anyway he intends to dress them all from head to toe in orange. He plans to stay in his forties forever, and cannot decide whether he is more comfortable in board shorts or a tuxedo. Happiest when sunbathing, he would gladly redecorate Michael McConaughey's beachside trailer so long as the owner gave him some help, shirtless. Stacy is a former life guard who just happens to be rather creative. She longs to be thinner, though fantasises about sharing her office with her own personal chef and admits that her waffle iron gives her absurd amounts of pleasure. Her grandmother taught her never to complain; in 10 years time she is planning a lot more holidays.

Bittman
HOW TO COOK
Peck Atlas of Human Anatomy for the Artist
Modern Furniture
GARDNER'S
Art through the Ages

Susan Salisbury & Jessica Earle

Designers: Susan Salisbury & Jessica Earle.
Company: Classic Country Pub Design, Berkswell, Warwickshire.
Profile: Design of bars, pubs, restaurants and hotels in the UK. Current projects include a boutique hotel and conference centre in Stratford upon Avon and a country pub in Guildford, Surrey.

THE FARM
No Bull

Wannabe cowgirls formerly known as Warthog and Wingnut respectively (though do not tell anyone). Jessica is a Radio 2 listener who wishes she had a bigger bottom. Most comfortable in her jeans and biker jacket, she likes nothing better than a good cry in front of The Bridges of Madison County. Susan would like a body out of Sports Illustrated and will not forgo plastic surgery if needs must. She still remembers the time as a child when she made her first den and knew she wanted to get into interior design. Both consider the Pyramids long overdue a refurbishment and would like to nominate the Benedictine monk Dom Pérignon for sainthood.

Ileana Dimopoulou Cadena

Designer: Ileana Dimopoulou-Cadena.
Company: Ileana Dimopoulou-Cadena Design Associates LLC, Athens, Greece.
Profile: Nine associates specialising in private residences and the occasional yacht in Greece, plus some restaurants and boutiques. Current projects include a villa on Mykonos Island, and a luxury brand's boutique in a new shopping mall in Athens.

For Ileana, becoming a designer has bee
has left her without enough hours in the
standards of her clients, she loathes clu
perfectionist she is never happy, and as
knows that she should work harder at p
she sees nothing but houses, houses, ho
interesting man in her husband of 25 ye
cheese eaten for breakfast on her roof t

a slow, fatal attraction, and one which
y. On a mission to improve the living
and minimalism in equal measure. As a
meone who always speaks her mind she
c relations. When Ileana shuts her eyes
es. When she opens them she sees an
. Perfection is a piece of Anthotiro soft
ace in the Greek Islands.

Yasumichi Morita

Designer: Yasumichi Morita.
Company: Glamorous Co. Ltd, Hyogo, Japan.
Profile: Japanese company which specialises in commercial design: recent projects include a watch shop in Tokyo, a French bistro in Nagoya and a Shinto shrine in Saitama, Japan.

Most productive in the afternoo
much for questionnaires. He co
feature, and reckons that the tv
age. One day he will design the

s, this designer does not care
iders his company his best
of them are improving with
ast word in retirement homes.

Laura Brucco

Designer: Laura Brucco.
Company: Laura Brucco, Buenos Aires, Argentina.
Profile: High end residential design, often for high profile individuals. Recent work includes apartments in Buenos Aires and houses in its outskirts.

Here is a wannabe icon with a love o
the latest technology. She dreads no
dismantling of ephemeral constructio
designer she would not exist, she dr
house in Punta del Este, Uruguay, ar
collecting small ornaments as clutte
dark chocolate, she listens to Bossa
considers the Nespresso coffee mac

noble materials and a respect for
ng, and only resents the daily
. Insisting that if she were not a
ms of building a breathtaking beach
she wishes that people would stop
uts her in a bad mood. Addicted to
va when she wakes up and
e a design of the Gods.

Michael Clattenburg

Designer: Michael Clattenburg.
Company: Michael Clattenburg Interiors, LLC, Dubai.
Profile: A small interior design office of no more than seven staff members whose projects are predominantly residential and located in Dubai. Some projects have taken them as far as France, Switzerland and Sweden.

A decorator so trusted by his clients that they will let him take decisions without their approval, Michael refers his own employees to a staff handbook to eliminate any grey areas in the office. His attitude is to eliminate the excess but decorate the boring, and he relies on a mixture of chemistry and courtesy to bond with his customers. With a love/hate relationship to clutter and an ear for Mozart in his waking hours, Michael has little routine and his inspiration does not keep time.

Ruth Levine and Andrea D'Cruz

Designers: Ruth Levine and Andrea D'Cruz.
Company: RLD, Paddington, New South Wales, Australia.
Profile: A mid-sized company with a mix of project types: high end luxury residential, hospitality, and commercial. Recent work includes a residential development by the waterfront of Rushcutters Bay in Sidney, and the interior decoration of a boutique hotel in downtown Sidney.

Andrea is a paper-dodger for whom a fresh mango equals happiness. She sees her work as the icing on the cake; Ruth sees hers as life transforming. Andrea would not touch a client if she did not sense a mutual trust and respect. Ruth prefers it when they say 'Here is a cheque, a key, and see you in three months.' Both dream of relocating the office to an industrial site: Andrea to a warehouse with soaring ceilings and an abundance of natural light, Ruth to a boathouse on Sidney Harbour. For Ruth, Byron Bay is the most beautiful place on Earth; Andrea would be content anywhere in the world so long as it entailed wearing skis.

Anemone Wille Våge

Designer: Anemone Wille Våge.
Company: Anemone Wille Våge Interior Design, Oslo, Norway.
Profile: A small creative team of three, dealing in high end residential projects, restaurants and hotels around Scandinavia and Europe. Work in progress includes a house in St Tropez, a hotel in Sweden and a mountain lodge in Norway.

AND·PET
BERNSTORFF
MDCCXCV

At night, when the telephones stop rir
best, dreaming up the next life-enhan
refurbishment of the Hotel Plaza Athé
university whilst furtively skimming Ho

ng, softly spoken Anemone is at her
g project, be it an airborne office or a
in Paris. Inspiration came to her at
e & Garden during lectures.

With natural curls that take her fro
bad, and with fantasies of being a
become accustomed to fresh coffe
morning by her husband. The sme
heavy sea air takes her back to the
her childhood in the deep fjords of

good hair days to
pera singer, she has
served in bed every
f honeysuckle and
ummer evenings of
orway's west coast.

Kate Kingston

Anna Lewis

Designers: Kate Kingston & Anna Lewis.
Company: Kingston Shaw, Birkenhead, UK.
Profile: A full service interior design practise with offices in the North West of England, London and Dubai. Projects in the residential, commercial and hospitality sectors. Recent work includes the refurbishment of a 10 bedroom house in the North of England, and a 19 bedroom castle hotel in Ireland.

Kate may be over-sentimental (a trait inherited fro
various business accolades. Considering herself th
Queen a job as her personal assistant, and to sha
a wish to be thinner, she once stole her father's ca
punishment she had to redecorate his house. Anna
want to age gracefully. At times she doubts hersel
listen to her clients to know she is doing alright (th
Delighted with the way she can transform an envi
and of reinventing Britain's caravan parks.

er mother) but she has still managed to scoop up earer of great style, she would like to offer The n office with a magician. A frustrated actress with nd drove to Mexico for the weekend; as a ears skinny jeans and high heels but does not the middle of a good idea, but she only has to gh her brother thinks she just draws all day long). nent, she dreams of playing Baby in Dirty Dancing

Catherine Grenier

Designer: Catherine Grenier.
Company: Atelier de Catherine, Madrid, Spain.
Profile: A team of five dealing in the interior design of offices, showrooms, restaurants, spas and hotels, with the occasional private residential project, working in Spain, Italy and the Caribbean. Current work includes the development of an own-brand furniture line, and the interior design of a hotel in Santiago de Compostela.

d'Anne-Marie
REINE DE SABA
Gateau au chocolat
Pour 8, il faut :
gr de farine
gr de beurre
gr de chocolat
gr de sucre
Mélanger farine, chocolat
sucre, jaune d'oeufs et
beurre. Ajoutez 1 pincée de
sel aux blancs d'oeufs.
les en neige ferme.
Incorporez-les délicatement
à la pâte. Versez dans un
moule beurré.
200 gr de crème fraiche
un peu de lait
2 ou 3 sachets de sucre
vanillé, 1 glaçon.
Rouler les
revenir dans

A long-haired garden-dwelling chair enthusiast with a tendency to treat her clients like boyfriends and her staff with a velvet glove, Catherine has grown from an undisciplined child with a flair for mathematics into an ideas woman with a sixth sense. That her mind will go blank is her biggest dread; that her creativity is limited by budgets is her biggest gripe. For Catherine, clutter and commercialism are daily struggles. With gluttony named as her biggest vice, and her husband pencilled in as her personal assistant, she still harks back to the wisdom of innocence she had as a child, when her biggest fear was her terrifying piano teacher.

Rosa May Sampaio

Designer: Rosa May Sampaio.
Company: Rosa May Decoracao de Interiores, Sao Paulo, Brazil.
Profile: Recent work includes a farm in Argentina, a penthouse in Rio de Janeiro and a resort in Bahia, Brazil.

Sensitive, respected and responsible, Rosa has not cried for seven years. For her the smell of rain on grass, the sound of the ocean, the sight of the beach; fashion and trends are of little consequence. Wedded to her spectacles, negligent of her health, and no longer in possession of her dreams, she could redecorate the Copacabana Palace Hotel in Rio or relocate her family to the beach in Uruguay, but only nature can fulfil her soul.

Jordi Vayreda

Designer: Jordi Vayreda.
Company: Jordivayredaprojectteam, Spain.
Profile: Team of five designers working on residential and commercial design, plus product and furniture design. Recent work includes the refurbishment of a 150 year old school, and the development of a range of lamps to be launched in 2009 in Milan.

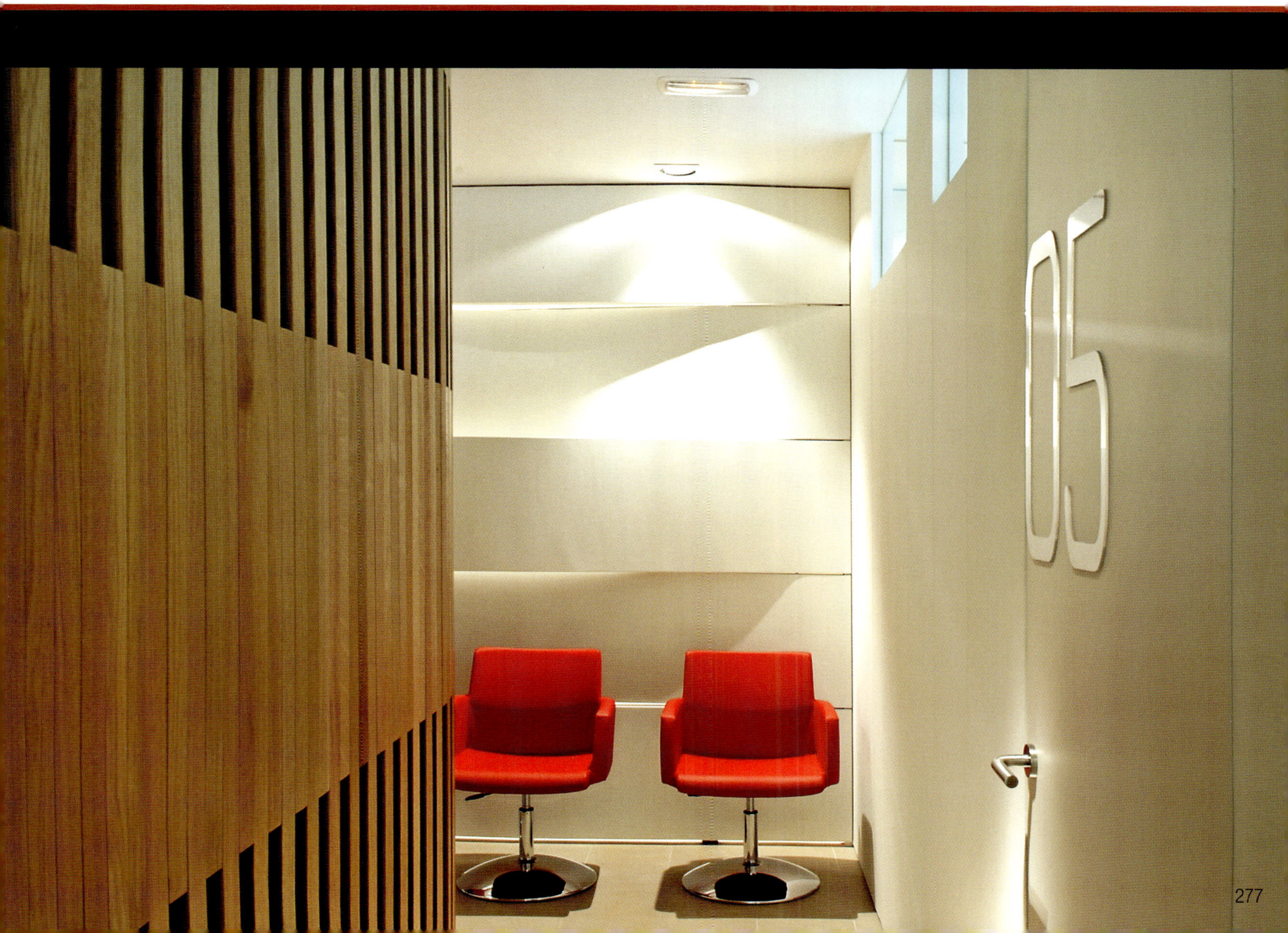

Ten years ago Jordi started his career i
maintaining his work ethic, and is marr
assistant, Sylvie. A Marlboro smoking p
housing in developing countries, he bel
is striving to be remembered as a gooc
a football pitch for his two small sons,
that they are not fit for school. Offsprin
him to do anything, he often finds it ha

design; ten years on he is happily with two children to his first fist with a desire to build sustainable es in professionalism in the office, and an. He has turned his roof terrace into h of whom try to persuade him daily f artistic parents who never forced to disagree.

Yvonne Jones & Andrew Burch

Designers: Yvonne Jones & Andrew Burch.
Company: Chameleon Interior Design Ltd, Cardiff, Wales, UK.
Profile: Practise established for 25 years specialising in high end international and residential properties in the private sector, as well as some exclusive commercial commissions. Recent work includes a Notting Hill townhouse and a listed country house, while current projects include a cliff top holiday retreat in Ireland and a luxury apartment in Majorca.

Yvonne is a frenetic optimist who lives and breathes her work. Andrew likes to bring order to this busy and chaotic world through slick, stylish interiors. Both place quality above quantity and wish that money was not always such an issue. At work they encourage closeness and enjoy a good group hug. Neither could contemplate life without their personal assistant; late deliveries bring them out in a cold sweat; full inboxes make them shudder. Yvonne wears her moods on her face; Andrew likes to care and share and tends to be freakishly neat. For him Neil Armstrong demonstrated that anything was possible. For Yvonne a house is nothing without the people who live in it.

Kamini Ezralow

Designer: Kamini Ezralow.
Company: Intarya, London.
Profile: A full-service interior design practice for the high end residential sector. Recent work includes an apartment in Mayfair and a terraced house in Kensington, while current projects include a super yacht, and a palace in Saudi Arabia.

Catch Kamini if you can: precise and to the point, her frenetic timetable leaves her pushed to expand. Ruling over a newly named company with a firmly gripped scale rule, she takes her inspiration from the embroidered Asian textiles of her mother's saris. Banishing clutter for fear that it will muddle her mind, she thinks that the key to successful decorating is in the detail.

Şeyhan Özdemir & Sefer Caĝlar

Designers: Seyhan Özdemir & Sefer Caĝla
Company: Autoban, Istanbul, Turkey.
Profile: Commercial and residential internationally. Recent projects include the new AFM Cinema in Istinye Park, Istanbul and the Istanbul Suites hotel.

Dynamic and chaotic, Sefer h
hold of his life and turn into a
energy and motivation, he is
unashamedly ambitious. Wed
Istanbul, he could not counte
consider working in anything

s watched his hobby take
career. Imbuing his team with
ceasingly productive and
ed to his home town of
nce moving, nor could he
ut design.

A visit to Naples eleven years ago left him stirred up by the smell of fried calamari. Sick to the teeth of minimalism, he finds himself calm and relaxed around disorder.

Louise Bradley

Designer: Louise Bradley.
Company: Louise Bradley, London.
Profile: Slick London operation comprising two showrooms and a clutch of bespoke private residential projects worldwide. Recent projects span a sky rise duplex apartment in Dubai and a private house in Grosvenor Square.

Louise is a team builder who dreads too many questions when she walks into the office. She would like to be remembered for making glamour comfortable, and hopes she will be wiser when she turns fifty. For her, clutter confuses the purpose of action, exercise is anathema and imitation is inferior. She could not imagine life without her wire haired dachshund, Marni.

Helene Forbes Hennie

Designer: Helene Hennie.
Company: Hennie Interiors, Oslo, Norway.
Profile: Specialising in high end residential work, plus hotels and offices. Recent projects include a house in Stockholm and an apartment in Antibes. Current projects include a country hotel outside Copenhagen.

Last year's Designer of the Year would like to be remembered as a good mother first, a designer second. Wedded to her drawing pad and pen, she is at peace in her cabin by the ocean and would like nothing better than to stay just the way she is. For her, family and friends are her biggest comfort, the team at work her biggest support.

Jake comes from a line of perfect Serbs but the sight of his tummy still makes him cry. Given half a chance he would dress his office in Star Trek uniforms and relocate to the Starship Enterprise. Happiest when watching makeover shows on television, he would like his mother to be his personal assistant - she always agrees with him. His tall and skinny partner René is an unabashed neat freak with an unanswered calling to the priesthood. He once heard angels speaking to him in a Design School interview, but today prefers ABBA Gold, red cabbage, and brown trainers.

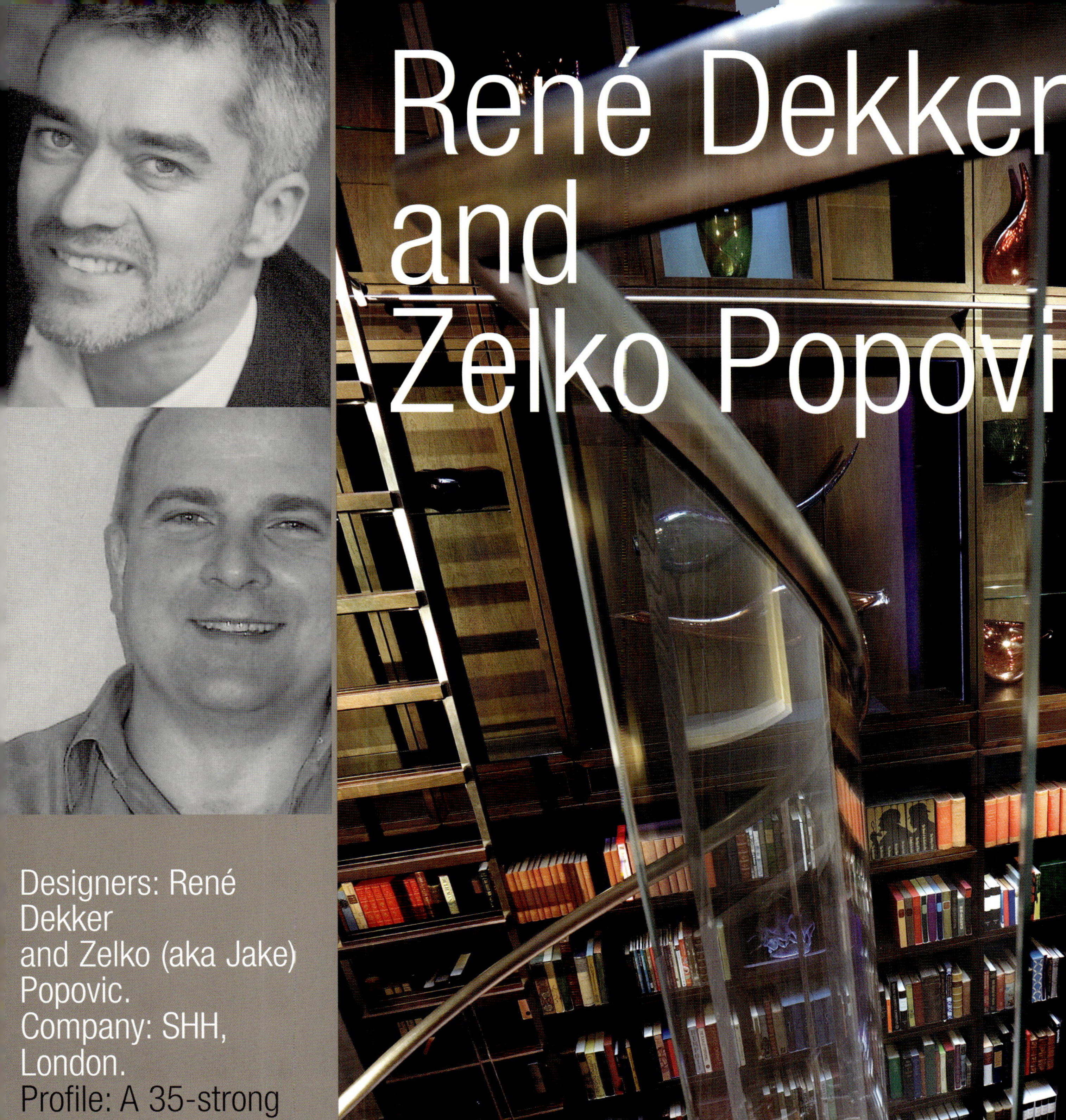

René Dekker and Želko Popovic

Designers: René Dekker and Zelko (aka Jake) Popovic.
Company: SHH, London.
Profile: A 35-strong architecture and design consultancy based in the West End of London working in both residential and commercial design. Current projects include a new-build restaurant in Bahrain, homes in Russia and Italy and a number of hotels in Lithuania.

Natalia Megret

Designer: Natalia Megret.
Company: Studio Bellevue, Moscow.
Profile: A small, rapidly growing company working predominantly in Russia and France on private residences, offices and spas. They are currently working on a number of large Moscow penthouses.

Wearing white linen in summer, white cashmere in winter, Natalia feels obliged to look stylish at all times. Describing her decorating style as luxurious elegance, she thinks of work as her religion and every project as an extraordinary adventure. Dreading design homogeny, she is as full of praise for the Soviet designed cast iron mincing machine as she is for the work of Philippe Starck. A gourmand by birth, a librarian in a previous life, and a ballet dancer in an alternative one, she would breakfast every day on caviar whilst listening to retro Soviet songs, and only really functions properly after several cups of coffee.

Rabih Hage

Designer: Rabih Hage.
Company: Rabih Hage, London.
Profile: A small team of highly qualified interior designers and architects creating unique residential interiors, high profile offices and boutique hotels in the UK and internationally. Recent work includes a speed boat concept and an environmentally friendly basement extension and interior, while current projects include a revolutionary luxury boutique hotel and an itinerant exhibition pavilion.

With his giraffe neck that keeps his head in the skies and his big feet that hold him perfectly stable, Rabih likes to think of himself as more of an interior alchemist than an interior designer. Working with small touches like a painter on canvas, aged 7 he sold a cartoon that he had drawn, to a friend for £5 and realised that he might have a lucrative future ahead of him. (He spent the proceeds on sweets and pornography). He has a weakness for chocolate fondant cake and would like to dress Anne Robinson in a pink uniform from Agent Provocateur and have her as his assistant. Planning to launch his design for the anti-gravity city scooter from the Eiffel Tower, he wishes everybody would stop saying 'darling' and that he was not so reliant on his Blackberry.

Broosk Saib

Designer: Broosk Saib.
Company: Broosk Saib, London.
Profile: One man band specialising in private, international residences. His recently completed work includes a bachelor pad in Eaton Square and a family holiday home in St Tropez.

Laid back and bespectacled, Baghdad born Broosk (Brooski to his friends) would like to nominate his assistant for sainthood - it is only Olivia who knows what to do with the little piles of clutter that he hoards behind his curtains. Early on in his career he almost lost a friend over a bad incident with some sofa fabric, but today, apart from dreaming of falling off a very tall building, this decorator is perfectly relaxed, particularly since earning a nod of approval from his late father.

CHATEAU DE FIEUZAL
GRAND CRU CLASSE
1986

Katharine Pooley

Designer: Katharine Pooley.
Company: Katharine Pooley Ltd, London.
Profile: Small team of designers headed up by Pooley with a predominantly private clientele. Recent work includes various high end London town houses, while the design of around 100 houses in an exclusive area of Moscow is currently keeping them rather busy. In the pipeline is the decoration of the new VIP suites at Heathrow, Terminal 5.

Former Harrods sales assistant is now destined for world recognition. In Pooley's book you work hard, you play hard, you think for yourself. Her childhood was filled with adventure and the smell of Tarmac, her adult life is punctuated by the sound of aeroplanes and compliments about her tummy button. Her staff smile when she comes into the room, her garden wilts when she so much as looks at it. Living under a flight path she never remembers her dreams but longs to demolish Heathrow Terminal 1 and replace it with something more inspiring.

soleil dans un verre

Meryl Hare

Designer: Meryl Hare.
Company: Hare & Klein, Woolloomooloo, Australia.
Profile: Small Australian practise dealin in the design of private residences, small resorts and developments internationally. Recent projects include a resort spa in Fiji and a new-build large family house on Sydney Harbour

Kind, democratic and most p
deadline, Meryl is at ease wi
- she is unusually tall. Happi
eating oysters and caviar, sh
house in Fiji and spend her

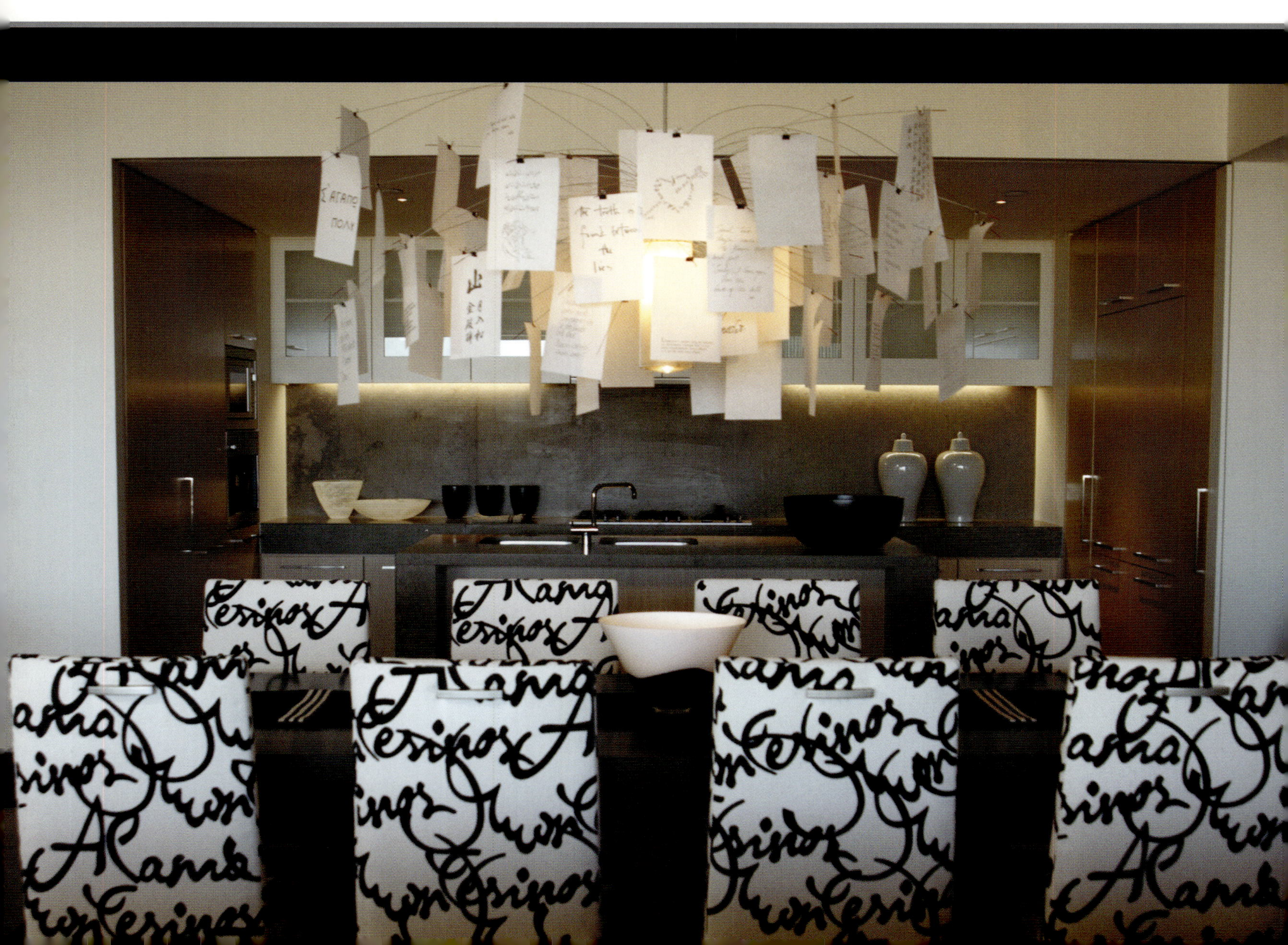

oductive an hour before
her staff looking up to her
st with her family, preferably
would like to build a tree
ys gazing at the sea.

For her, shared laughter is the
and client, though she did onc

truest bond between designer
make a client cry with joy.

Mirka McNeill Farmer

Designer: Mirka McNeill Farmer.
Company: Living Room, London.
Profile: High end residential projects in the UK and Poland, plus commercial projects including boutique hotels and show flats. Recent residential projects include the renovation of two listed properties in Warsaw; currently working on the redesign of a Victorian house in London.

Degree-laden decorator with an eye for a derelict building; Mirka would like to be remembered for breathing new life into old buildings and has her sights set on decorating a castle - the older the better. Working alone she has the luxury of not talking to anyone in the morning, and only wishes that sometimes she might remember to skip a meal. At peace on the Caribbean Coast, at odds with bureaucracy, and at her best in a simple black dress, or single-sculling along the Thames.

Karen Howes and Gail Taylor

Designers: Karen Howes and Gail Taylor.
Company: Taylor Howes, London.
Profile: A multi-disciplined, international practice working on hotels, spas, show apartments and private residences. Recent work includes the Meyrick Hotel in Galway and a show apartment in London's Bishops Avenue. Currently working on the home of a celebrity chef and the 50 storey Vauxhall Tower.

Established Award winners big on communicating but have banned emails on Fridays. Super-efficient, they are busy building an empire with a team they treat as family. Karen's personal assistant is her best friend; her youngest child is forever rearranging her bedroom. Gail's daughter makes her cry when she sings, and her grandfather taught her a thing or two about kindness. Both would like to be taller, spend more time in France, and design the ultimate English country house. Neither can stop themselves talking about the 'Wow factor', nor can they define exactly what it is.

Christopher Dezille

Designer: Christopher Dezille.
Company: Honky, London.
Profile: Boutique design practice specialising in high concept interior design and architectural projects for both property developers and private individuals. Currently working on a ski chalet in Courchevel, France and a private residence in Belgravia.

Christopher is an early-rising big thinker who would like to be considered one of the most influential designers of his generation. He sees his relationships with his clients as love affairs, his team of colleagues as an orchestra, his day as a blank canvas. He spends his nights awake and his days in search of perfection. Sunglasses, wine, watches and trainers are his vices, consideration his virtue. He once spent three days working in a butcher's shop.

Launderette

金鎖匙
大紅袍

Alison Vance & Jeff Laing

Designers: Alison Vance & Jeff Laing.
Company: Jeffreys Interiors, Edinburgh.
Profile: Small company with a retail showroom and a design practice, working on middle to top end private projects with some small scale commercial ones. Recent work includes a holiday house in North Berwick, and a penthouse in Edinburgh, while current projects include the refurbishment of a large stately home and the refit of a house in Northern Ireland.

Here are a pair of life-embracing Highlanders, happiest on a Friday night and dreaming of the day when Scotland will enjoy a more Mediterranean climate. Alison is considering plastic surgery, and has noticed her own skinny legs in her children's. Jeff is rejoicing in his latest project - the refit of a lingerie shop - while doing his best to avoid paperwork. Both intend to be walking their dogs in 10 years time, and both would like to be anywhere in the world right now but Donegal.

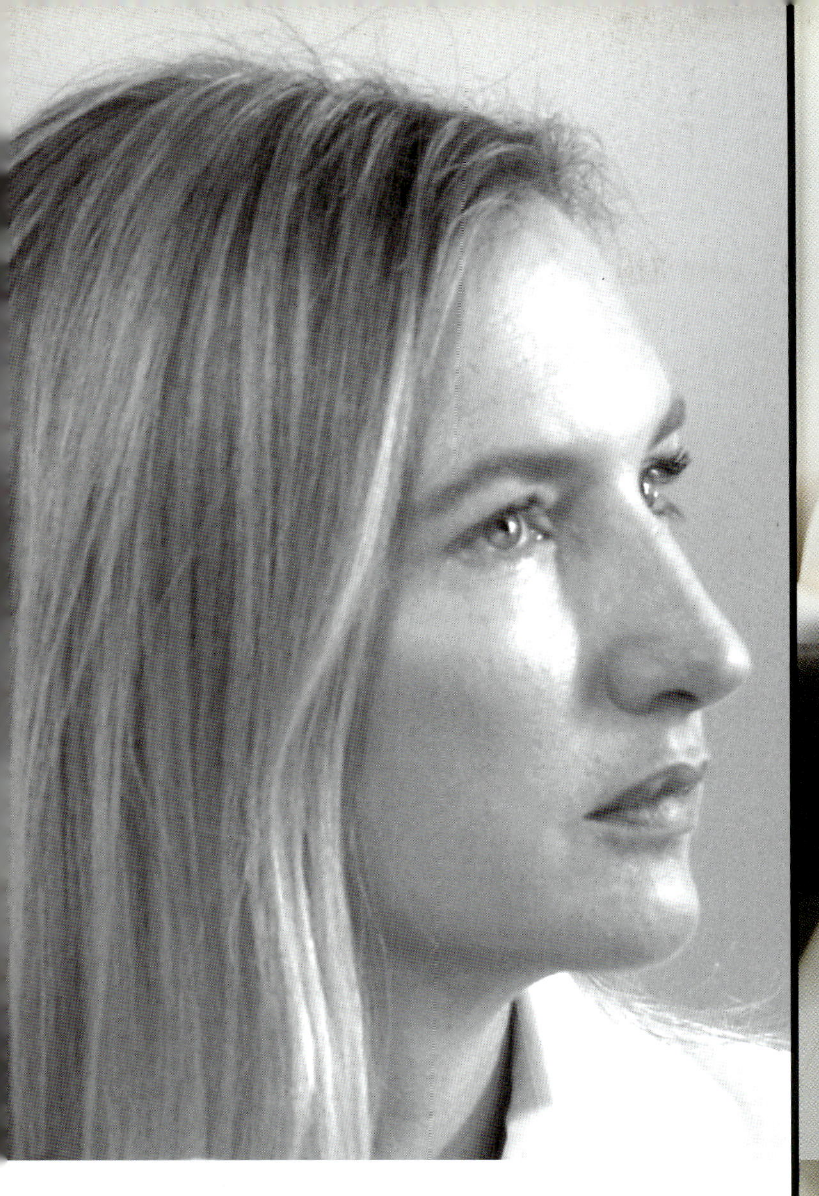

Federica Palacios

Designer: Federica Palacios.
Company: Federica Palacios Design, Geneva.
Profile: Small, international practice working on private houses and boutique hotels. Recent work includes Hotel Post in Zermatt and several chalets in Gstaad.

Instinctive cowboyboot wea
dreads looking at her in-bo
chauffeur. A childhood in Ar
around leather, while her ba
her Swedish grandmother.

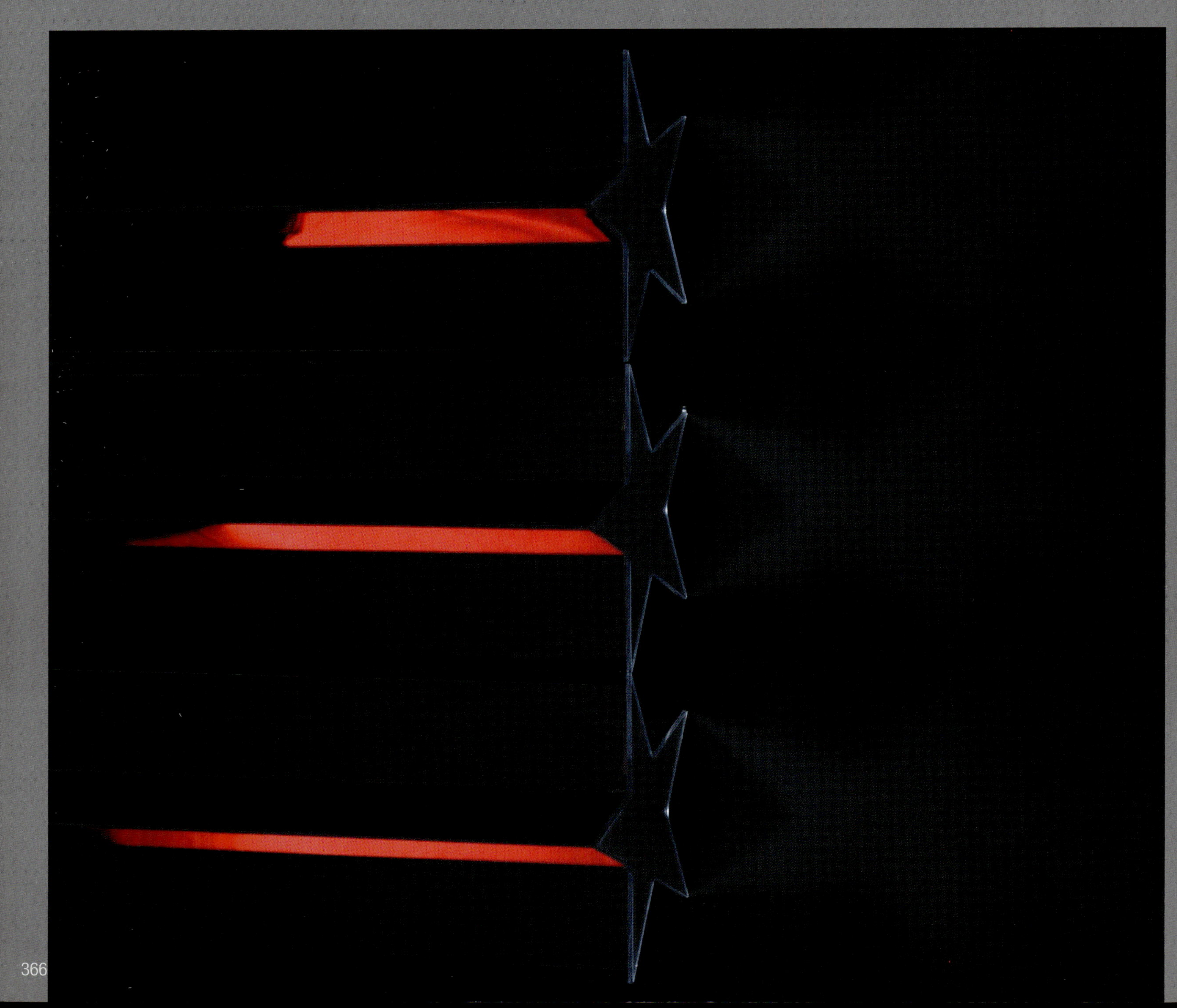

g mother of three who
and dreams of having a
entina has left her nostalgic
ng skills were learnt from

Inseparable from her mobile phone, incapable of quitting smoking, in love with Keanu Reeves, she has a thing about the Maldives and would never consider going to a party with a theme.

Chris Browne

Designer: Chris Browne.
Company: Conservation Corporation Africa, South Africa.
Profile: Africa's largest luxury ecotourism and safari operator, of which Chris Browne is Creative Director, specialising in designing small luxury safari lodges. Currently working on projects in Kanha national park in India, Sabi Sands in South Africa, and a safari lodge in Botswana.

Chris is a risk-taking adventurer who once had rather a thing about power tools. Determined to create environments conducive to good sex, he dreams of fighting jihads against boring people, and of dressing his office in Vivien Westwood. He sees perfection in his wife, the ideal PA in Gisele Blunden, and the office as a place to have fun. He thinks people are surprised when they meet him that he is not more serious, and he believes his wife when she says he has a nice ass.

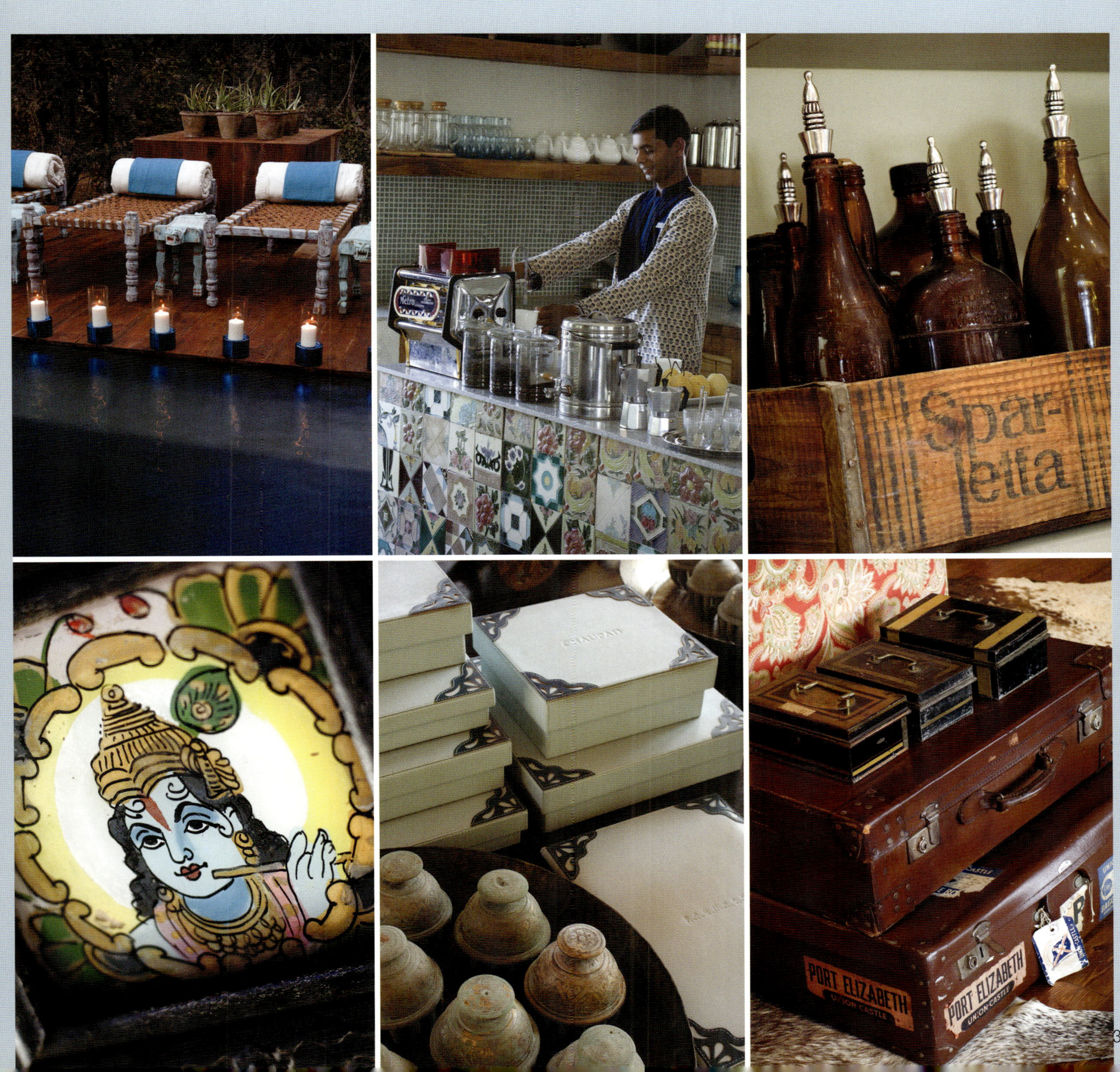

Mr Foo Fatt Chuen

Designer: Mr Foo Fatt Chuen.
Company: Axis Identity Group, Kuala Lumpur.
Profile: One of the largest design practices in Malaysia with offices in Kuala Lumpur, Dubai and Shanghai, offering design consultancy and construction management. Projects are predominantly in the commercial sector: hotels, restaurants, offices, serviced apartments and fitness centres.

A former newspaper delivery boy, Foo (Fudge to his friends) sees himself as setting standards in a design world marred by Postmodernism. Thanking his father for his penchant for French wine, and his fifth year architecture teacher for taking him down the path he now treads, he likes to keep things neat and tidy, particularly when it comes to his window box. A Pink Floyd fan and scuba diving enthusiast, the dark side of the moon and crystal clear waters give him equal amounts of pleasure.

THE OLIVE
THE OLIVE

Zeynep Fadillioglu

Designer: Zeynep Fadillioglu.
Company: Zeynep Fadillioglu Design, Istanbul, Turkey.
Profile: International interior decorator whose recent projects include a luxurious ten suite hotel, Les Ottomans, in Istanbul.

Zeynep is a perfectionist day dreamer who spent 10 years designing restaurants for her husband before realising she could take it up professionally (and get paid for it). She once swam the Bosporus from Europe to Asia, and would like to fly her office from Istanbul to London at will. As a child she climbed onto a glass roof with her cousin Rifat Ozbek to watch a strip show and ended up being hospitalised. Her ideal morning is spent in silence eating white Turkish cheese.

Jayne Wunder

Designer: Jayne Wunder.
Company: Jayne Wunder Interior Design, Cape Town, South Africa.
Profile: Small company working on commercial and private projects: residential homes, boutique hotels, restaurants and bars. Recent work includes the interior of an aeroplane and a series of upmarket homes in Cape Town and Johannesburg.

Meet Jayne, an undomesticated, generous spirit with good ears who likes to think she gives her clients light and space in which to grow. Happiest in her pyjamas, or at work among empowered women, she is frustrated at not being properly used and would never willingly share an office with anyone. The smell of hops and malt take her back to a childhood spent eating porridge and reading Winnie the Pooh.

Monica Melhem & Anne Bazan

Designers: Monica Melhem & Anne Bazan.
Company: Monica Melhem, Capital Federal, Argentina.
Profile: Projects are predominantly residential, with an international client base.

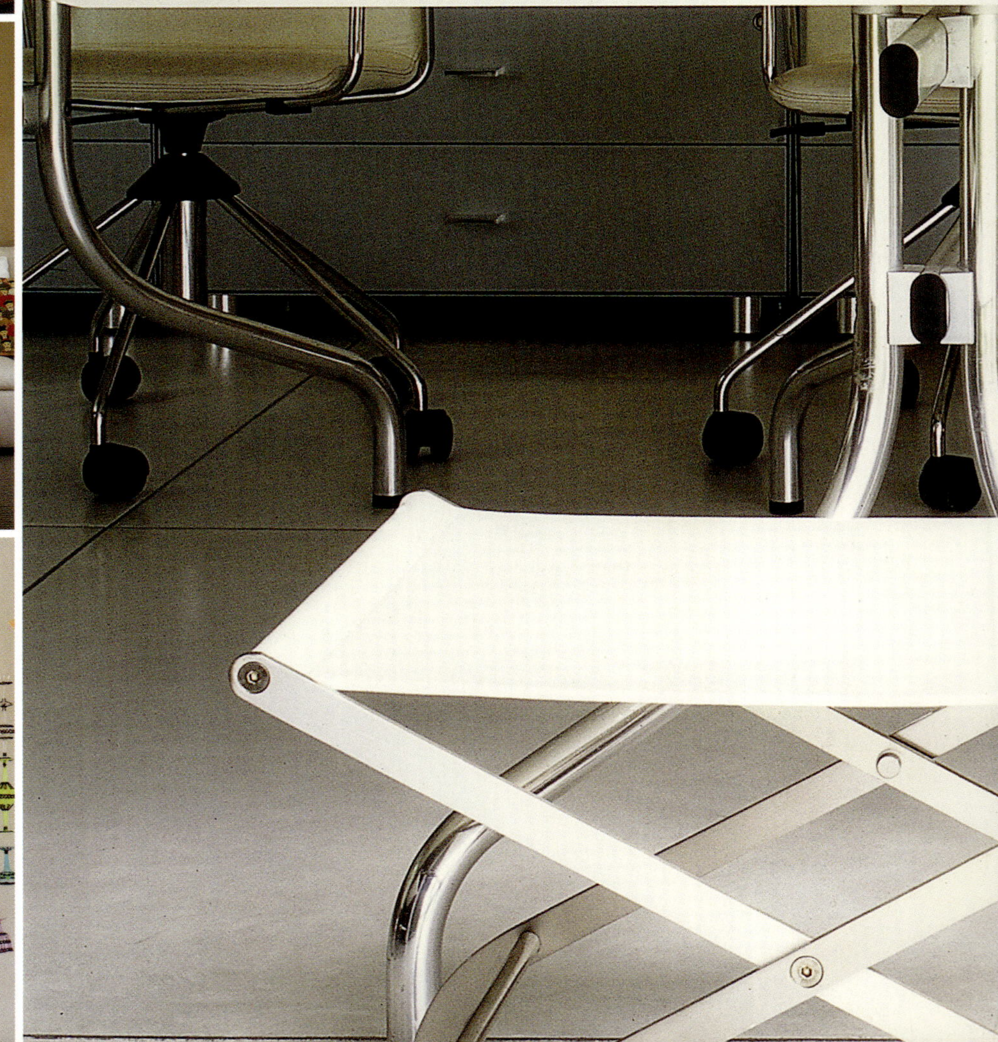

An hourglass Argentinian who likes nothing better than a client coming back for more, Monica dreads disorder and expects unblinking attention at the office. Having inherited a tendency towards obsessive perfectionism from a serial criminal in the family, she would willingly go at your clutter with a vacuum cleaner. Anne is a young-at-heart mother of many who is at her most comfortable in jeans and a T-shirt. A patriotic polo enthusiast, she can think of no better place to live and work than Argentina, but wishes she was free of limitations. Regularly over-exposing herself to the sun, she treats all of her clients as celebrities and sees every trend, good or bad, as opening the mind. Pity her children: they all want to be decorators.

Christian Baumann

Designer: Christian Baumann.
Company: Abraxas Interieur, Switzerland.
Profile: Small company taking on high end private and some commercial projects all over Europe. Current work includes three private houses in the Zurich area.

Upbeat, undisciplined and extreme, Christian works best under pressure and surrounded by women. Best in the early hours of the morning, his taste in black cloaks lends him a Dracula-like demeanour, and the thought of an unsexy client fills him with dread. He has banned ugly shoes and silly walks from the office and he would ideally like to dress his staff in Agent Provocateur.

Dismissive of domestic app
tolerant of clutter, he would
assistant and build a versio

ances, and reluctantly
ake Marie Antoinette as his
of Versailles in the desert.

Ligia Casanova

Designer: Ligia Casanova.
Company: Atelier Ligia Casanova, Lisbon, Portugal.
Profile: Private commercial architecture and interior design projects internationally, including a hospital and complex of apartments in the South of Portugal, a hotel and restaurant in the North, and a loft in Antwerp.

Intuitive and organised, casua
designer she would be an astr
into space with an assistant tc
of demolishing the cemented
Hyperactive as a child and nic
is still addicted to chocolate a

nd quirky, if Ligia weren't a
naut. She dreams of flying
ake care of the red tape, and
burbia of her home town.
named 'Skinny' at school, she
l the nickname has not stuck.

mamá

She would like to propose a ban on all toxic materials, and blames most of what is wrong with this decade on the nouveaux riches of the Eighties.

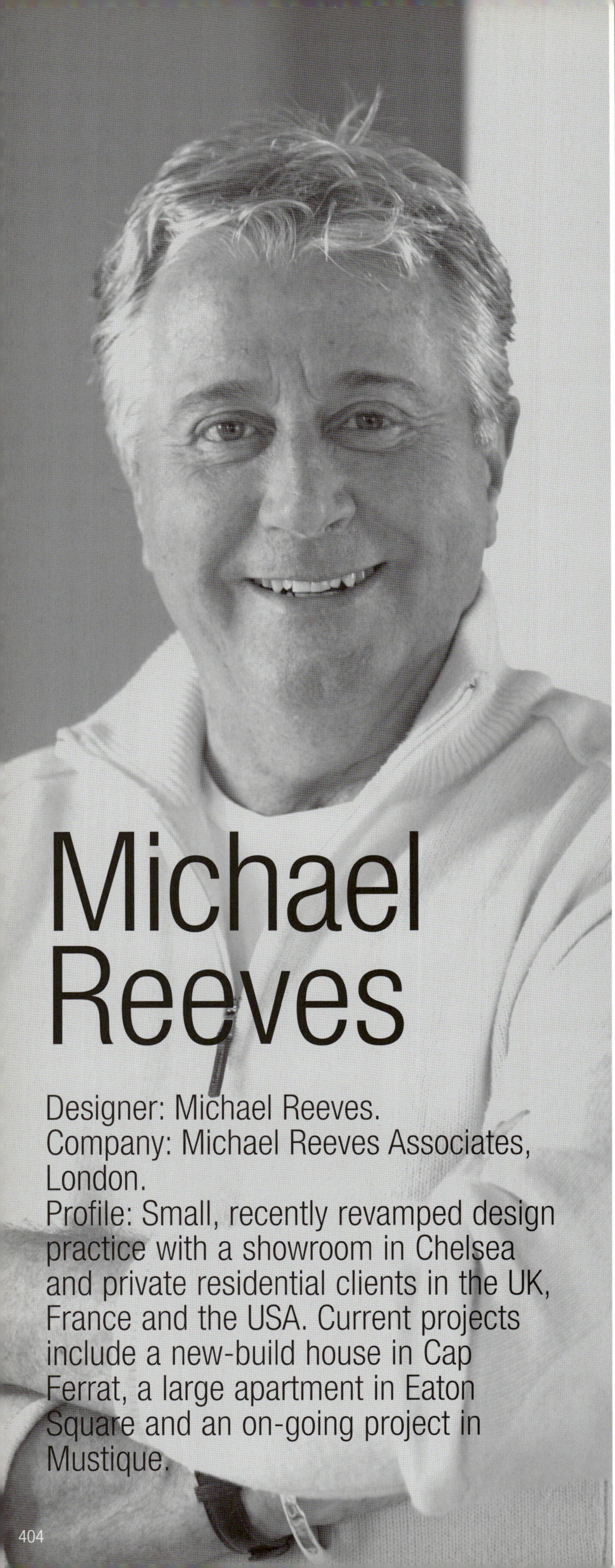

Michael Reeves

Designer: Michael Reeves.
Company: Michael Reeves Associates, London.
Profile: Small, recently revamped design practice with a showroom in Chelsea and private residential clients in the UK, France and the USA. Current projects include a new-build house in Cap Ferrat, a large apartment in Eaton Square and an on-going project in Mustique.

A professional tweaker who is most productive after his early morning run, Michael finds estimates a nuisance and clutter a sickness. Happy in Prada jeans with a stomach full of Marmite on toast, he thinks 'lifestyle' is overused and Art Nouveau an abomination. Hooked on shopping and deeply attached to his Burmese Buddha, he cries at the opera and is still getting over the moment when his father unexpectedly sold the family piano.

João Mansur

Designer: João Mansur.
Company: João Mansur Arquitetura & Design, Sao Paulo, Brazil.
Profile: Small practice which carries out private and commercial projects across Europe and the Americas. Recent work includes the restoration of a 19th century farmhouse in the state of Sao Paulo and beach houses in Trancoso, Bahia.

João is a blonde-loving, anxiety-prone father who lets out his emotions to relieve his soul. A one-time swinger, the smell of Patchouli takes him back to happy times in London in the 1970s. At 58 he feels that his body is ageing quicker than his mind, though he would never consider plastic surgery. Proud of his ability to size up a space and its potential at first glance, he intends to leave a legacy behind him and has been planning his dream home since he was a boy. With designs on living in London, New York or Paris, today he lives in Sao Paulo where he is cultivating a penthouse topiary garden.

PAZ
CENTURY
REMBRANDT

Silvio Rech, Lesley Carstens & Ink Design

Designer: Silvio Rech.
Company: Silvio Rech Architects and Ink Design Lab, Johannesburg, South Africa.
Profile: Recent work includes the Ngorongoro Crater Lodge in Tanzania and an extensive design on North Island, a private island in the Seychelles.

An open-minded creative pioneer who believes as much in a building's aura as its interior, Silvio sees himself standing in the place where design, lifestyle and ideologies meet. For him each project has its own DNA and architecture is simply the stage set for beautiful thoughts and a feeling of freedom. By combining African handcrafting with cutting edge design he is inventing a new language, and transcending the tedious boundaries of normality. In 1998 he employed his first assistant, Leslie. She is now his partner and they have 2 children together. He recently insisted his staff grew moustaches over the weekend. He cries daily. He throws his toys in the pasta if it is not al dente. Admin makes him over eat and gives him heart burn. He would just like to be left alone with his imagination.

Steve Leung

Designer: Steve C.T. Leung.
Company: Steve Leung Designers Ltd, Hong Kong.
Profile: Large architecture and design company employing over 250 staff and specialising in large commercial projects, office buildings, residential, show flats, shopping malls and hotels. Currently working on Maison Baccarat in Macau, the Hyatt Regency in Yiwu and a restaurant project in Dubai.

Tirelessly driven brand builder
and requires his staff to dress
If he was not a designer he w
takes him back to a childhood
whom inspired him to become
planning a black-themed Hallo

who sleeps without dreams
in black on formal occasions.
uld be a nobody. Stinky tofu
spent with his uncles, both of
the man he is today. He is
ween party at the office.

Dedicated to his family, though s he has not been out into his gar year and he cannot tolerate mes

eldom at home,
en for over a
y environments.

Erik Møyland Andersen

Designer: Erik Møyland Andersen.
Company: Interior Plus, Stockholm, Sweden.
Profile: Small company working on a mixture of high end private and commercial projects. Recent work includes a large apartment in Stockholm and the total refurbishment of a 1920's villa at Steninge Slott.

Happiest after being fed, Erik would like to dress his office in proper Lycra bunny outfits, and likes them to scream with fear whenever he comes into the room.

In an ideal world he would share his room with a patisserie chef, something that may interfere with his wish to turn himself from chubby cheeks to chubby chic. He celebrates his 29th birthday yearly at his country house, dressed in casual cashmere and stripey socks, but underneath the layers he is still the precocious child he was at five.

4 Kit Kemp
Firmdale Hotels
18 Thurloe Place
London SW7 2SP
Tel 020 7581 4045
Fax 020 7589 0100
kitkemp@firmdale.com

14 Jan des Bouvrie
Ontwerpstudio Jan des Bouvrie
Kooltjesbuurt 11
1411 R.Z. Naarden
Holland
Tel 0031 35 699 6219
Fax 0031 35 632 1574
info@hetarsenaal.nl

20 Erin Martin
Martin Design
1118 Hunt Avenue
St Helena
CA 94574
Tel 001 707 963 4141
Fax 001 707 963 4146
erin@erinmartindesign.com

24 Zaha Hadid
Zaha Hadid Architects
10 Bowling Green Lane
London EC1R OBQ
Tel 0207 253 5147
Fax 0207 251 8322
press@zaha-hadid.com

32 Douglas Mackie
D Mackie Design Ltd
8 Holland Street
London W8 4LT
Tel 0207 937 1051
Fax 0207 937 1052
douglas@dmackiedesign.com

36 Aleksandra Laska
Ola Laska Ul.
Krakowskie Przedmiescie 85 M.5
00079 Warsaw
Poland
Tel/Fax 0048 22 826 0796
Mobile 0048 609 522 942
olalaska@neostrada.pl

46 Fiona Barratt
Fiona Barratt Interiors Ltd
World's End Studios
132-134 Lots Road
London SW10 ORJ
Tel 0207 349 7090
Fax 0207 349 7091
info@fionabarrattinteriors.com

54 Brian Gluckstein
Gluckstein Design
234 Davenport Road
Toronto
Ontario M5R 1J6
Tel 001 416 928 2067
Fax 001 416 928 2114
briang@glucksteindesign.com

58 Angelos Angelopoulos
Angelos Angelopoulos
5 Proairessiou Str
11636 Athens
Greece
Tel 0030 210 756 7191
Fax 0030 210 756 7191
design@angelosangelopoulos.com

64 Amanda Kaye & Lisa McCartney
LK Interiors
Ebenezer Chapel
Bradden Lane
Gaddesden Row
Herts HP2 6JB
Tel 0845 130 1372
Fax 0845 130 1382
inspireme@lkinteriors.com

70 Philip Tang, Brian Ip
P Tang Studio Ltd
Rm 603-604 Harry Industrial Building
49-51 Au Pui Wan Street FO Tan N.T.
Hong Kong
Tel 00 852 2669 1577
Fax 00 852 2669 3577
office@ptangstudio.com

74 Sandra Nunnerley
Sandra Nunnerley, Inc.
41 East 57th Street
New York NY 10022
USA
Tel 001 212 826 0539
Fax 001 212 826 1146
sandra@nunnerley.com
www.nunnerley.com

80 Sue Rohrer
Sue Rohrer SA
Gstadstr 11, 8702 Zollikon
Switzerland
Tel 0041 79 207 9093
Fax 0041 44 919 0288
sue@suerohrer.com
www.suerohrer.com

86 Mr Patrick Leung
PAL Design Consultants Ltd
23A Neich Tower
128 Gloucester Road
Wanchai
Hong Kong
Tel 00852 2877 1233
Fax 00852 2824 9275
hongkong@paldesign.cn

90 Ekaterina Medvedeva
Geometry
Kutuzovskiy prospect 45
Moscow 121170
Russia
Tel/Fax 007 495 771 70 41
gilk@rdm.ru
www.geometry-moscow.ru

94 Nicholas & Christian Candy
Candy & Candy
100 Brompton Road, Knightsbridge
London SW3 1ER
Tel 0207 594 4300
Fax 0207 594 4301
info@candyandcandy.com
www.candyandcandy.com

100 Giano Goncalves
Ana D'Arfet
Rua Tenente Coronel
Sarmento 6/6A
9000-020-Funchal
Portugal
Tel 00351 291 757 998
Fax 00351 291 744 396
anadarfet@gmail.com

106 Eddy Doumas/Lisa Kanning
/Dana Hugo
Worth Interiors
PO Box 8369 (US Mail)
30 Benchmark Road # 103
(UPS/FedEx)
Avon
Co 81620, USA
Tel 001 970 949 9794
Fax 001 970 949 4252
eddy@worthinteriors.com

110 Flora Lau
Flora Lau Designers Limited
6A Hoi Bun Industrial Building
6 Wing Yip Street
Kwun Tong, Kowloon
Hong Kong
Tel 00 852 2893 8007
Fax 00 852 2893 8067
flora.lau@fldesigners.com.hk

116 Jan Showers
Jan Showers & Associates
1308 Slocum Street
Dallas, Texas
75207 USA
Tel 001 214 514 5492
Fax 001 214 747 5242
jennifer@janshowers.com

122 Stefano Dorata
Stefano Dorata Architetto
00197 Roma
23 Via Francesco Denza
Italy
Tel 0039 06 808 4747
Fax 0039 06 807 76 95
studio@stefanodorata.com

128 Kunihide Oshinomi
K/O Design Studio
2-28-10 # 105
Jingumae Shibuya-ku
Tokyo
Japan 150-0001
Tel 0081 3 5772 2391
Fax 0081 3 5772 2419
oshinomi@kodesign.co.jp

134 Dina El Khachab
& Hedayat Islam
Eklego Design Ltd
8, El Sheikh El Marsafy Sq
1st Floor
Apt. 4
Zamalek 11211
Cairo
Egypt
Tel 00202 273 66 353/357 274
Fax 00202 273 66353
eklego@eklegodesign.net

138 Maria Hovtun
Maria Interior Design
Slemdalsveien 43
0373 Oslo
Norway
Tel +0047 95890725
maria@mariainteriordesign.no
www.mariainteriordesign.no

142 Amy DePierre
Associates III
1516 Blake Street
Denver
Co 80202
USA
Tel 001 303 534 4444
Fax 001 303 629 5035
amy@associates3.com

148 Kris Lin
KLID
301 Room The Fourth Build
No 1163
Hong Qiao Road
Chang Ning District,
Shaghai
China
Tel 0086 21 620 999 28 & 628 396 05
Fax 0086 21 620 99 918
kl_iad@vip.163.com

154 Nadia & Georgy Ananiev
ABL Architecture & Design Bureau
b.Kozikhinskiy per.27
Building 1
Moscow 123001
Russia
Tel 007 495 699 8021
Mobile 007 910 484 5290
a-b-l@comtv.ru

158 Kathleen Hay
Kathleen Hay Designs
4 Witherspoon Drive
PO Box 801
Nantucket MA 02554
USA
Tel 001 508 228 1219
Fax 001 508 228 6366
kathleen@comcast.net

164 Joseph Sy
Joseph Sy & Associates
17th Floor
Heng Shan Centre
145 Queen's Road East
Wan Chai
Hong Kong
Tel 00852 2866 1333
Fax 00 852 2866 1222
design@jsahk.com

170 Daun Curry & Nicole Fuller
Vessper Wilde
425 West 23rd Street
Suite 7e
New York
NY 10011
USA
Tel 001 646 216 9185
Fax 001 646 224 8577
daun@vessperwilde.com
nicole@vessperwilde.com

174 Jean Turcotte & Louis Pepin
Atelier de L'Opera
1165 Ave Greene
Westmount Montreal
Quebec
Canada H3Z 2A2
Tel 001 514 935 6245
Fax 001 514 931 4316
atelierdelopera@bellnet.ca

178 Arch. Patricia Pedrazzi
Innolink-Ambient
Piazza San Giovanni
66925 Gentilino, Lugano
Switzerland
Tel 0041 79 620 4941
Fax 0041 91 9211 941
innolink-ambient@ticino.com

182 Pedro Guimarães
Pedro Guimarães LDA
Avenida Da Boavista 1503
4100-131 Porto
Tel 00351 226 096 069
Fax 00351 226 096 069
mpedroguimaraes@iol.pt

188 Ajax Law Ling Kit, Virginia Lung
One Plus Partnership Limited
9/F New Wing, 101 King's Road
North Point
Hong Kong
Tel 00852 2591 9308
Fax 00852 2591 9362
admin@onepluspartnership.com

192 Marta's
Marta Espregueira Mendes -
Arquitectura e Decoracao de
Interiores, Lda
Rua de Fez no 691
4150-331 Porto
Portugal
Tel 00351 22 617 84 32
Fax 00 351 22 617 7994
geral@martas.com.pt
www.martas.com.pt

196 Thomas Chan
Thomas Chan Designs Ltd
Unit 1706, Stelux House
698 Prince Edward Road East
Kowloon
Hong Kong
Tel 00852 2308 1280
Fax 00852 2308 1350
office@thomaschan.hk

202 Luciana Teperman
Luciana Teperman
Av. Nove de Julho 5966
cj42 01406-200
Sao Paulo, Brasil
Tel 0055 11 308 32 726
Fax 0055 11 3062 6950
luteperman@uol.com.br

206 Kiyofumi Yusa, Richard Lee
R & K Partners, Inc.
Architectural Design/Interior Design
ADEX Ichiban-cho 2F
22-3 Ichiban-cho, Chiyoda-Ku
Tokyo
Japan # 102-0082
Tel 0081 3 3263 9006
Fax 0081 3 3263 9007
randk@js8.so-net.ne.jp

210 Robert Walker
Alexander James Interiors
How Lane Farm, White Waltham
Berkshire SL6 3JP
Tel 0118 932 0828 & 0118 924 1602
Fax 0118 932 0886
robert@aji.co.uk
www.aji.co.uk

214 Kinney Chan
Kinney Chan & Associates
11F Chung Nam Building
1 Lock Hart Road
Hong Kong
Tel 00 852 2545 1322
Fax 00 852 2850 6099
www.kca.com.hk
christina@kca.com.hk

218 Jim Gauthier & Susan Stacy
Gauthier/Stacy Inc
112 Shawmut Avenue
Suite 6A
Boston
MA 02118
USA
Tel 001 617 422 0001
Fax 001 617 422 0011
info@gauthierstacy.com

222 Susan Salisbury & Jessica Earle
Classic Country Pub Design
Holly House
Spencers Lane
Berkswell
Warwickshire CV7 7BZ
Tel 01676 533 169
Fax 01676 535 012
pssalisbury1@hotmail.com

228 Ileana Dimopoulou-Cadena
Ileana Dimopoulou-Cadena Design
Associates LLC
Architectural Interior Design
& Decoration
13-15 Kyriazi Str
14562 Kifissia
Athens
Greece
Tel 0030 210 623 2614
Fax 0030 210 623 2615
cadenag@otenet.gr

232 Yasumichi Morita
Glamorous Co Ltd Interior Design,
Product Design
1F 7-6 Omasu-cho
Ashiya
Hyogo
659-0066
Japan
Tel 0081 797 23 6770
Fax 0081 797 23 6771
info@glamorous.co.jp

238 Laura Brucco
Laura Brucco
Museo Metropolitano
Castex 3217
1er Piso C1425 CDC
Buenos Aires
Argentina
Tel 005411 4808 9565
Fax 005411 4808 9565
laurabrucco@fibertel.com.ar
www.laurabrucco.com

242 Michael Clattenburg
Michael Clattenburg Interiors LLC
City Tower One
Office 303 Sheikh Zayed Road
P.O. Box 49235
Dubai U.A.E.
(& Tystagatan, Stockholm, Sweden)
Tel 00971 4 33 11 513
Fax 00971 4 33 11 594
info@michaelclattenburg.com

246 Ruth Levine & Andrea D'Cruz
RLD (Rldesign Pty Ltd)
2/10 Elizabeth Street
Paddington
NSW 2021
Australia
Tel 0061 2 9331 4066
Fax 0061 2 9331 8503
info@rldesign.com.au

252 Anemone Wille Våge
Anemone Wille Våge Interior Design
Dronning Astridsgt 7
0355 Oslo
Norway
Tel 0047 22 60 27 33
Fax 0047 22 60 56 32
anemone@anemone.no

258 Kate Kingston
Kingston Shaw Ltd
3 The Workshops
Marcus Street
Birkenhead CH41 1EU
Tel 0844 736 0141
Fax 0151 647 3215
contact@kingstonshaw.com

264 Catherine Grenier
Atelier de Catherine Sl
Calle del Tato, 17
28043 Madrid
Spain
Tel 0034 91 721 61 50
Fax 0034 91 721 61 51
cgrenier@atelierdecatherine.com

270 Rosa May Sampaio
Rosa May Decoracao de Interiores
Rua Alemanha 691, Jardim Europa
Sao Paulo SP
Brazil CEP 014 480 10
Tel 005511 308 51092
Fax 005511 306 12810
rosamaysampaio@terra.com.br

274 Jordi Vayreda
Jordivayredaprojectteam
Mont Salvatge 32
17,800 Olot (Girona)
Spain
Tel 0034 972 27 18 49
Fax 0034 972 26 65 57
info@jordivayreda.com

280 Yvonne Jones & Andrew Burch
Chamelion Interior Design Ltd
62 Cathays Terrace
Cardiff
CF24 4HY
Tel 029 2037 1277
Fax 029 2023 1497
info@chamelioninteriors.com

284 Kamini Ezralow
Intarya
48 Old Church Street
London SW3 5BY
Tel 0207 349 8020
Fax 0207 349 8021
kamini@intarya.com

292 Seyhan Özdemir,
Sefer Câglar
Autoban
Tatarbey 2 No. 1
K.2 Galata 34425
Istanbul
Turkey
Tel 0090 212 243 8642
Fax 0090 212 243 8640
info@autoban212.com

298 Louise Bradley
Louise Bradley
15 Walton Street
London SW3 2HX
Tel 0207 589 1442
Fax 027 589 2009
enquiries@louisebradley.co.uk

304 Helene Hennie
Hennie Interiors
Thomlesgt 4
0270 Oslo
Norway
Tel 00 47 22 06 85 86
Fax 00 47 22 06 85 87
post@hinteriors.no

310 René Dekker & Zelko Popovic
SHH
1 Vencourt Place
Hammersmith
London W6 9NU
Tel 0208 600 4171
Fax 0208 600 4181
renedekker@shh.co.uk

314 Natalia Megret
Studio Bellevue
14/9 Malyi Levshinsky per
Moscow
Tel 007 495 991 6010
Fax 007 495 637 5949
bellevue@list.ru

318 Rabih El Hage
Rabih Hage
69-71 Sloane Avenue
London SW3 3DH
Tel 0207 823 8288
Fax 0207 823 8258
info@rabih-hage.com

322 Broosk Saib
Broosk Saib
4 Heathrise
Kersfield Road
London
SW15 3HF
Tel 0208 788 5130
Fax 0208 788 5130
broosksaib@aol.com

330 Katharine Pooley
Katharine Pooley Ltd
160 Walton Street
London, SW3 2JL
Tel 0207 584 3223
Fax 0207 584 5226
pout@katharinepooley.com

336 Meryl Hare
Hare & Klein
138 Cathedral Street
Woolloomooloo
NSW 2011 Australia
Tel 00612 9368 1234
Fax 00612 9368 1020
enquiries@hareklein.com.au

342 Mirka McNeill Farmer
Living Room
22 Elm Grove Road
Barnes
London SW13 OBT
Tel/Fax +44(0) 208 878 2641
Mobile +44(0) 7974 207592
mirkamcneill@gmail.com
www.mirkamcneill.com

348 Karen Howes & Gail Taylor
Taylor Howes Designs Ltd
29 Fernshaw Road
London SW10 OTG
Tel 0207 349 9017
Fax 0207 349 9018
admin@thdesigns.co.uk
www.thdesigns.co.uk

354 Christopher Dezille
Honky Ltd
Unit 3, 40-48 Bromells Road
London
SW4 OBG
Tel 0207 622 7144
Fax 0207 622 7155
info@honky.co.uk

360 Alison Vance
Jeffreys Interiors
8 North West Circus Place
Edinburgh EH3 6ST
Tel 0131 247 8010
Fax 0845 88 22 656
alison@jeffreys-interiors.co.uk

364 Federica Palacios
Federica Palacios Design
14 Grand Rue
1204 Geneva
Switzerland
Tel 0041 22 310 2276 Fax 0041 22
310 2286
federica@federicapalaciosdesign.com

370 Chris Browne
Conservation Corporation Africa, CC
Africa
Postal address:
Private Bag x 27
Benmore 2010 Johannesburg
South Africa
physical address:
Block F Katherine Street
Sandown
Tel 0027 11 8094 300
Fax 0027 11 809 4511
chris.browne@ccafrica.com

374 Foo Fatt Chuen
Axis Identity Group
Penthouse North Block
Wisma Selangor Dredging
142-D Jalan Ampang
50450 Kuala Lumpur
Malaysia
Tel 00 603 2163 4181
Fax 00 603 2163 4186
foo@axisidentity.com

378 Zeynep Fadillioglu
Zeynep Fadillioglu Design
Ahmet Adnan Saygun Cad
No 72 D5 34340 Ulus
Istanbul
Turkey
Tel 0090 212 287 0936
Fax 0090 212 287 0994
zeynep@zfdesign.com
design@zfdesign.com

382 Jayne Wunder
Jayne Wunder Interior Design
4 Cardiff Street
Newlands, Cape Town
South Africa 7700
Tel 0027 21 67 44 936
Fax 0027 21 674 4937
jwunder@mweb.co.za

386 Monica Melhem & Anne Bazan
Monica Melhem
Av Libertador 2902 ~ 12
1425 Capital Federal
Argentina
Tel 0054 114 802 7994
Fax 0054 114 802 5762
monicamel@fibertel.com.ar

392 Christian Baumann
Abraxas Interieur
Hegibachstr. 112
CH-8032 Zurich
Switzerland
Tel 0041 44 392 21 92
Fax 0041 44 392 21 93
info@abraxas-interieur.ch

398 Ligia Casanova
Atelier Ligia Casanova
Rua Artilharia Um
32 - r/c esq
1250-040 Lisboa
Portugal
Tel 00351 919 704 583
Fax 00351 213 955 630
ligia.casnova@sapo.pt
www.ligiacasanova.com

404 Michael Reeves
Michael Reeves Associates Ltd
30 Old Church Street
London SW3 5BY
Tel 0207 351 6515
Fax 0203 055 0111
info@michaelreevesassociates.co.uk
www.michaelreevesassociates.co.uk

408 João Mansur
João Mansur Arquitetura & Design
R. Groenlândia 19228 B
Jardim America
São Paulo SP
Brasil 01434-100
Tel 0055 11 3083 1500
Fax 0055 11 3081 7732
joaomansur@joaomansur.com

414 Silvio Rech & Lesley Carstens
Architecture & Interior Architecture
INK Design Lab
32B Pallinghurst Road Westcliff
Johannesburg
South Africa
Tel 0027 82 900 9935
adventarch@mweb.co.za

418 Steve C.T. Leung
Steve Leung Designers Ltd
9/F Block C, Sea View Estate
8 Watson Road, North Point
Hong Kong
Tel 00852 2527 1600
Fax 00852 2527 2071
Mobile 00852 6113 1244
sla@steveleung.com
www.steveleung.com

424 Erik Møyland Andersen
Interior Plus
Grev Turegatan 57
SE-114 38 Stockholm
Sweden
Tel 0046 8 665 31 18
Fax 0046 8 665 31 19
erik.andersen@interiorplus.com

Editor: Martin Waller
Text: Daisy Bridgewater
Project Executive: Annika Bowman
Product Design: Graphicom Design

First Published in 2008 by Andrew Martin International

Copyright © Andrew Martin International
All rights reserved.
No part of this book may be reproduced, stored in a retrieval system or transmitted in any form or by any means, electronic, electrostatic, magnetic tape, mechanical, photocopying, recording or otherwise, without the prior permission in writing of the publisher.

ISBN 978-0-9558938-0-3

Reproduction by Wellprint Ltd.
Printed in Singapore by Craft Print International Ltd.

Acknowledgments

The author and publisher wish to thank all the owners and designers of the projects featured in this book.

They also thank the following photographers:

Simon Brown, Kees Roelofsen, Dominique Vorillon & Cindy Anderson, Courtesy of Silken Hotels & Roland Halbe Fotografie & Steve Double, Gary Hamill, Hanna Dlugosz & Aleksandra Laska, Tom Scott, Ted Yarwood, Vangelis Paterakis, Warren Smith photography & J. Tarbox at Fotografix, Ulso Tsang & Philip Tang, Miguel Flores-Vianna & Jaime Ardiles-Arce, Reto Guntli, PAL Design Consultants Ltd, Vladimir Klyosov & Elena Koldunova, Candy@Candy, Antonio Moutinho & Miguel Costa, The Estico Group & Kim Sargent, Joseph Cheung & Pazu Chu & Derek Que, Dominique Vorillon & Stephen Karlisch & Jeff McNamara, Giorgio Baroni, Nacasa & Partners, Second Wind Tokyo, Faouzi Massrali, Studio Vest/Stine & Siv Naero, Dave Marlow, Lv Bao he, Dmitry Livshitz/AD Russia, Jeffrey Allen, Joseph Cheung & Pazu Chu & Derek Que, Peter Margonelli/Jill Lotenberg/Luis Da Cruz, Robin Hill, Lorenzo Nencioni, Francisco de Almeida Dias, Chengdu sales office & Gzlakes Guanghou, & Guanghou sales office, Marta Espregueira Mendes, Thomas Chan, Tuca Reines, Faouzi Massrali, Vince Hart & Charleschurch.com & Paul Eccleston, Arthouse Ltd & John Powell & Simon Wilson, Mr Kinney Chan, Sam Gray, Pank Sethi, Vangelis Paterakis & Vangelis Rokas, Nacasa & Partners, Daniela Mac Adden, Andrew Garner, Eddy Doumas, Werner Anderson & Espen Gronli & Dreyer Hensley & Mona Gundersen, Nicolas Laborie, Riccardo Labougle, Allain Brugier, Eugeni Pons, Pep Sau, Jordi Vayreda, Sergi Farres, Raul Franch, Albert Font, Phil Boorman Photography Ltd, Richard Waite, Ali Bekman, Ray Main, Morten Andenaes, Hans Fonk, Boris Bendikov, Brian Benson, www.marcuspeelphotography.co.uk & www.philipvile.com, Andy Hendry at 2 Cs Communications Ltd, Jenni Hare, Andreas von Einsiedel, Marcin Czechowicz for Dobre Wnetrze, Michal Mrowiec, Hugo Burnard & Tim Evans Cook, Warren Smith photography & J. Tarbox at Fotografix, Chris Tubbs, Wayne Vincent, Rob McDougal, Dook, Lin Ho & Jack Shea, Korayv Erkaya, Mark Williams, Virginia de Guidice, Marco Blessano, Manuel Gomes da Costa, Andrew Twort, Beto Riginik & Paulo Madeira, David Ross (courtesy of Visi magazine, SA) Michaela Shuter, Silvio Rech, Mr Ulso Tsang & Pazu Chu, Magnus Magnusson & Magnus Anesund.

All transparencies and/or photographs reproduced in the book have been accepted on the condition that they are reproduced with the knowledge and prior consent of the Photographer concerned, and no responsibility is accepted by the Publisher or Printer for any infringement of copyright or otherwise arising out of publication thereof.